THE ROCK ISLAND LINE

Railroads Past and Present
George M. Smerk, Editor

A list of books in the series appears at the end of this volume.

ROCK ISLAND LINES
ANNUAL REPORT 1960

THE
ROCK ISLAND
LINE

BILL MARVEL

INDIANA UNIVERSITY PRESS

Bloomington and Indianapolis

This book is a publication of

Indiana University Press
Office of Scholarly Publishing
Herman B Wells Library 350
1320 East 10th Street
Bloomington, Indiana 47405 USA

iupress.indiana.edu

Telephone orders   800-842-6796
Fax orders   812-855-7931

Manufactured in China

Cataloging information is available from the
Library of Congress.

ISBN 978-0-253-01127-5 (cloth)
ISBN 978-0-253-01131-2 (eb)

1 2 3 4 5 18 17 16 15 14 13

Front cover: E8 No. 648 rattles the diamonds
at Joliet Union Station, 40 miles out of La Salle
Street, with the *Peorian*. In April 1971, No. 12
still offers dining car service between La Salle
Street and its namesake destination. *Ed Kanak*

Endpapers: This system map shows Rock Island's
reach at its full extent, in the 1950s when lines
stretched from South Dakota wheatlands deep
into bayou country and from Lake Michigan
to the New Mexico desert. Surprisingly much
remains today, operated either by regional carriers
or by onetime merger prospect Union Pacific.
Author collection

Frontis: In 1960, the Rock issued their annual
report with this spectacular cover art. *Author
collection*

Title pages: Making a wonderful clatter, U28B
No. 256 leads the eight units on Train 82 away
from Denver on February 2, 1969. The show of
force is unnecessary, since the eastbound line is
mostly downhill, but traffic imbalances often leave
surplus units at the western end of the system. *Bill
Marvel*

Back cover: Bumped from jockeying passenger
cars, its main work since it was built by EMC in
1942, SW1 No. 536 has been sold to Producers
Grain in Amarillo and still finds useful work
kicking rusty grain hoppers around an elevator in
Plainview in the Texas Panhandle. *Tom Kline*

For Donna

The Rock Island Line is mighty good road
The Rock Island Line is the road to ride.

—ATTRIBUTED TO HUDDIE WILLIAM (LEAD BELLY) LEDBETTER

CONTENTS

THE
ROCK ISLAND
LINE

INTRODUCTION & ACKNOWLEDGMENTS

I grew up amid railroads. Great-grandpa Marvel finished out his career as a Colorado & Southern conductor five years before I was born. Burlington's 38th Street Yard was just a vacant lot from my grandparents' back porch. Union Pacific's Denver–Cheyenne trains hustled past my great-aunt's house in suburban Henderson. Rio Grande's big 3600-class "malleys" were a constant presence on family fishing trips and vacations. When we moved from West to East Denver, the sound of slamming boxcars in Rio Grande's Burnham yards was exchanged for the nightly departure of UP's Kansas Division mixed. Through my open bedroom window I could always tell whether a steamer or a diesel was in charge.

But the Rock Island was an exotic stranger. It rolled into town from across the High Plains, from places I could only guess

at. My first encounter came while I was watching a softball game with my father. A rumble arose from behind the grandstands and I turned just in time to see one of Rock's magnificent red and maroon TAs trundle by from the Burnham roundhouse, on its way to Union Station to take the *Rocket* east.

I never forgot that apparition. So naturally, when I turned my attention to railroads in a serious way, the Rock Island was a favorite. Other fans hung out at the C&S, which was still switching Rice Yard with steam, or headed down to the Joint Line for the parade of C&S and Santa Fe freights and the daily passage of Missouri Pacific's *Eagle*. I was as likely to point the hood of my battered '49 Ford east, to Sandown or Sable or Strasburg, where, if I was lucky, Rock Island FTs or FAs, or even an exotic BL2 would be on the move. What a great way to run a railroad, I thought,

never realizing that it was because of poverty that Rock was still running first-generation power when every other road in town had moved on to GP20s and -30s.

This book, in a way, is the story of that poverty and how and why it came about.

To help tell the story I leaned on the work of more than a dozen photographers, some of them shooting buddies, others known only by reputation and the quality of their work. All came through gloriously, as these images show. The bylines will identify them, but I owe special thanks to Ron Hill, Dale Jacobson, and Paul Dolkos, with whom I have had the pleasure of sharing happy days at trackside. Ed Seay Jr. and Lloyd Keyser dug into their personal collections. The others whose work is displayed on these pages went

to great lengths to provide the images I asked for, entrusting me with irreplaceable slides. Many went to the trouble of scanning images and sending me discs. Thanks, gentlemen—this is as much your book as mine.

Eunice J. Schlichting, chief curator at the Putnam Museum in Davenport, Iowa, and Coi Gehrig at the Denver Public Library Western History Collection smoothed the way to those important collections. The DeGolyer Library at Southern Methodist University provided a refuge, a reading room, and access to one of the best railroad libraries in the country. Victor F. Kralisz, manager, Humanities and Fine Arts Divisions of the Dallas Public Library, made precious writing space available in that library's writer's room when my dining room table overflowed.

Some liked it, some loathed it, but the railfan-designed bicentennial paint scheme for E8A No. 652, the *Independence*, looked better than the patriotic costumes that adorned most other roads' diesels in 1976. The year after the whoopla, the unit oozes steam on a frigid February morning as it makes a quick station stop at Joliet. *Dan Tracy*

CHAPTER ONE

THE BRIDGE

The Chicago, Rock Island & Pacific Railroad began, fittingly, with a journey across the Mississippi River. The small group of prosperous businessmen was crossing by boat, not bridge. That would come soon enough. For the moment they were focused on a swifter, more modern kind of transportation: a railroad. The year was 1845, and on this sultry June afternoon, they were headed from the Iowa to the Illinois side for a meeting with the wealthiest and most powerful man in the region, Colonel George Davenport.

The first Rock Island bridge, between its April 21, 1856 completion and May 6—when the steamboat *Effie Afton* struck just right of the draw span, setting the bridge on fire. A contemporary view of the Iowa side shows the draw span, right, and bustling Davenport, left, where Antoine LeClair donated his house and land for Rock Island's station and yard. *Putnam Museum of History and Natural Science, Davenport, Iowa*

CITY OF DAVENPORT . IOWA.

Davenport beckons from across the Mississippi in this 1858 Rufus Wright lithograph depicting the arrival four years earlier of the first Rock Island train in its namesake city. Steamboats *Ben Campbell* and *Tishomingo* stand offshore. By 1856, a bridge will span these waters. *Putnam Museum of History and Natural Science, Davenport, Iowa*

Davenport had been railroad-minded ever since 1839, when he and a 300-pound half-Potawatomi Indian named Antoine LeClair laid out the town that would bear Davenport's name. Canals were fine, and Davenport had promoted his share. However, they froze in winter and were subject to drought and flood in summer. A railroad, on the other hand, could reach out from canals and rivers, link them, and even cross them. A network of railroads was already racing across the land from Baltimore. Soon it would reach

Chicago. If riverfront towns like Rock Island and Davenport were to thrive, they too would have to reach out, not just downriver to St. Louis, but east to Chicago and eventually to the West, where the nation was headed. Iowa's population was already 96,088; in a year and a half, it would be a state.

The little group from across the river must have had something like this in mind as members stepped ashore and made their way to Colonel Davenport's mansion. Separated from mainland Illinois by a narrow stretch of river called "The Slough," Rock Island had been the site of an army fort until 1836, and much of it was still federal property. But with a population of 4,000, the town was growing.

Packed into Davenport's parlor that evening were LeClair—a crowd by himself—

who operated a ferryboat on the river; attorney James Grant; lawyer and banker Ebenezer Cook; and miller and real estate promoter A. C. Fulton. All were from the Iowa side. W. A. Whittaker and Lemuel Andrews were Rock Island businessmen. Charles Atkinson, who had platted the town of Moline, and N. D. Elwood, who had ridden the stagecoach all the way from Joliet, rowed across The Slough from the Illinois mainland to attend. With them was Richard P. Morgan, a civil engineer with some experience in railroads. The men talked late into the night and, when they emerged, they had agreed to send Lemuel Andrews to the state legislature at Springfield to obtain a charter for a railroad company. The line was to reach 75 miles from Rock Island to the banks of the Illinois River at La Salle. From there, boats of the Illinois and Michigan Canal would connect with Chicago.

Eight years before, the Illinois legislature appropriated the then-enormous sum of $10 million for a package of internal improvements that included canals, bridges, and a railroad network. However, a financial panic that year killed that ambitious scheme. Now, a more cautious legislature waited almost two years before issuing a charter to the Rock Island & La Salle Rail Road Company. Capital stock was set at $300,000, and a board of commissioners was chosen to oversee sales.

Almost four years passed before the needed capital was raised from local farmers and businessmen along the proposed route. With the money finally at hand, in November 1850, the commissioners met in Rock Island and elected directors of the new railroad. Two weeks later the directors elected James Grant president. Colonel Davenport did not live to see his dream realized; within weeks of the June 1845 meeting, he was murdered in his home by robbers.

Grant's first task was to find someone to build the road. With several directors in tow, he traveled to Chicago where he sought out Henry Farnam, who was just building the Michigan

Southern Railroad westward toward Chicago. One of the most brilliant civil engineers the young Republic had produced, Farnam had experience laying out and building canals and railroads in the East, and he understood that the future lay with rails. The new venture appealed to him. Almost immediately he set out on horseback to scout the proposed route. When he returned, he told directors he would build their railroad, provided the line extended from the Mississippi River not just to the banks of the canal at La Salle, but all the way into Chicago, where it would meet the rails of the Michigan Southern. The result, he pointed out, would be a continuous line of railroad from the Mississippi to the Atlantic Ocean.

The directors agreed and dispatched Grant to ask the legislature in Springfield to amend the original charter to reflect the new destination. Legislators were reluctant. The Illinois and Michigan Canal Company had been built by the state; a railroad to Chicago would siphon off business. Finally, a

A landmark for decades for Rock Island commuters, the Chicago Board of Trade punctuates the scene at La Salle Street, where RS-3 No. 488 idles in July 1965, before the afternoon suburban rush. Boiler-equipped Nos. 485–499 were geared to run 80 miles per hour and outlasted most of their freight-hauling kin. *Donald Haskel*

Wearing the short-lived white wings paint scheme, U28B No. 249 is just three months old in June 1966, on its way west from De Pue through the lush Illinois River bottoms. *Terry Norton*

Opposite top: On its way to Burr Oak Yard on October 3, 1970, U25B No. 237 pauses at La Salle, Illinois, in the ancient heart of the Rock Island, to await a fresh crew. *Paul Dolkos*

Opposite bottom: SW1500 No. 944 is equipped with Flexicoil trucks and geared for 77 miles per hour, neither of which is useful here as the five-year-old unit shuffles cars at Armourdale in September 1971. The locomotive's usual assignment is to transfer drags among Kansas City's numerous rail yards. *Paul Dolkos*

compromise was reached: The railroad would pay a toll to canal operators on the traffic it carried between La Salle and Chicago. Farnam urged a reluctant Grant to accept the compromise. (As it turned out, the canal operators failed to approve the agreement by the deadline, and no tolls were ever paid.) On April 4, 1851, the directors approved the new charter, reincorporating the Rock Island & La Salle as the Chicago & Rock Island Rail Road. They asked the Iowa legislature to grant a charter for construction of a depot at Davenport—not coincidentally on land owned by Antoine LeClair. Clearly, their eyes were not only on Illinois.

With Henry Farnam had come a bonus: his astute and resourceful business partner, Joseph Sheffield. If the Rock Island was to build all the way to Chicago, 181 miles, it would need money, and plenty of it, and Sheffield had connections to eastern bankers. In August 1851, members of the railroad's executive committee met with Farnam and Sheffield in New York to negotiate a contract. The finished document reveals Sheffield's sharp pencil. The railroad company would buy the right-of-

way and fence it. Farnam and Sheffield would build and equip the entire line for $3,987,688. This lump sum would cover grading and track-laying, all rails and ties, bridges, stations, freight houses, engine houses, and 500 feet of docks on the Chicago riverfront. The work was to be completed by January 1, 1856.

The contract was signed in September. A shipment of iron rails arrived from England in December, and in April 1852, construction began in earnest, with Farnam personally overseeing the work.

The contract with Farnam and Sheffield meant that control of the railroad would rest not in the hands of the Illinois businessmen who had first promoted it, but in the portfolios of eastern bankers, the money men. In February, Michigan Southern track gangs spiked down the final 6 miles into Chicago. Those miles, by agreement, were to be jointly owned with Rock Island. By then, James Grant had resigned the presidency to devote his time to the Iowa legislature, where he was speaker of the house. In his place, directors elected John B. Jervis, a gifted civil engineer and Farnam associate who, like Farnam, had forged his reputation

Above: Split Rock Tunnel, 2 miles east of La Salle, Illinois, has long been abandoned as GP7 No. 1279 hustles past with an eastbound in September 1971. Piercing a bluff overlooking the Illinois River, the bore dates to 1851. *Terry Norton*

Opposite bottom: The westbound *Golden State* has drawn an interesting assortment of motive power this March afternoon as FP7 No. 402, an E7B, and an E3A lead the road's flagship past Silvis. *Terry Norton*

Overleaf: Running on former Great Northern rails, U25B No. 220 and GP40 No. 4705 work a transfer back to Rock Island's Inver Grove Yard in St. Paul on August 24, 1974. Burlington Northern's Westminster Tower, background, survived until 2003. *Ralph Back*

building canals and railroads in the East. A. C. Flagg of New York became treasurer.

With Farnam in command in the field and Sheffield watching the money, things began to move.

By October 10, rails reached Joliet, 40 miles out. A celebratory excursion was called for. On a blustery Sunday morning, a bright and beaming Rogers 4-4-0 named *Rocket* (not for Rock Island, but for the pioneering George

Stephenson locomotive that had hit 29 miles per hour in the famous 1929 Rainhill trials in England) pulled six yellow coaches from the new 22nd Street depot to Joliet, a two-hour journey on still-raw trackage. Because there was nowhere to turn the engine, the train was backed to Chicago, arriving in time for an evening banquet at the Sherman House. Regular service to Joliet, two trains a day, began a week later.

Sixty miles beyond Joliet, La Salle was less welcoming. By March, track gangs began to spike down rail along the foot of the Illinois River bluffs. In anticipation of the railroad's arrival, local entrepreneurs had been buying up property, but that property was on top of the bluffs. City council demanded that the railroad redirect its line and, and when the railroad refused, the council threatened to forcibly move the tracks. Male citizens were enjoined, under threat of a $10 fine, to lend *continued on page 18*

continued on page 18

By March 1973, Chicago's "Rocket House" no longer dispatched passenger power beyond the Mississippi River, but Peoria- and Rock Island–bound trains and suburban trains still fill the ready tracks this morning. Shown are E8A No. 649, E9A No. 660, and AB6 No. 750. *Kevin Piper*

continued from page14
their muscle to the removal effort. The dispute was settled only after the state legislature affirmed the railroad's right to build along the river bottoms.

That May, Sheffield and Farnam signed a contract with a group of local investors to build a railroad from Peoria to a connection with the Rock Island. They were joined in the project, called the Peoria & Bureau Valley, by an erstwhile physician turned speculator, Thomas Clark Durant. Only 33, Durant had bought and sold a lot of Rock Island stock.

With no further problems, rails reached Bureau by September and Sheffield in mid-October 1853. By Christmas, when severe weather halted construction, the railhead was only 23 miles out of Rock Island. Business was very good, and the contractors were calling for additional locomotives and cars.

Above: One of only two GP7s to get their noses chopped at Silvis, No. 1275 leads a pair of ex-UP F9Bs on a westbound manifest at Atalissa, Iowa, on a cold March afternoon in 1975. The F98s have just come off the Lafayette coal train. *John Dziobko*

Left: F7A No. 117 came down the old Burlington, Cedar Rapids & Northern on Saturday night. Now turned on the air-operated turntable and coupled to its train, the 25-year-old unit idles in the glow of a Sunday morning at Burlington, Iowa, on November 10, 1974, before setting out on the return trip to Columbus Junction. *Dick Hovey*

Rock Makes Tracks

With Rock Island rails advancing across Illinois, in February 1853, the Iowa legislature, meeting in Iowa City, granted three of the road's original founders—Antoine LeClaire, Ebenezer Cook, and A. C. Fulton—a charter to build another railroad. This new enterprise would reach from the banks of the Mississippi at Davenport across the state to Council Bluffs, and it would be called, logically enough, the Mississippi & Missouri Railroad. Capitalization was set at $6 million.

From the start, the M&M was created to continue the westward march of the Chicago & Rock Island. Besides LeClair, Cook, and Fulton, organizers included Rock Island's president, John B. Jervis; Farnam, who was the road's chief engineer and contractor; and Durant. Rock Island's treasurer, A. C. Flagg, became M&M's treasurer.

Eastbound at Colona, Illinois, GP7 No. 4517 gleams in Rock Island's "new image" blue-and-white scheme created by John Ingram. On June 8, 1975, the former No. 1274 is just three weeks out of the Capital Rebuild Program at Silvis shops. *Bill Marvel*

William Walcott, a Farnam associate, was placed in charge of acquiring right-of-way and looking into possible branch lines. His committee soon recommended that M&M build a branch south from Davenport to Muscatine and northeastward to Cedar Rapids and the Minnesota border. In June 1853, the charter was duly amended. On September 1, Antoine LeClair turned the first spadeful of earth in Davenport, and three days later a survey party led by Grenville Dodge began working westward. The surveyors arrived in Council Bluffs on November 22. Actual construction would not begin for a year and a half.

Across the river, however, track crews were busy. On February 22, 1854, citizens of Rock Island had something besides George Washington's birthday to celebrate. The first train from Chicago rolled up to the "passenger house" at 5 p.m., announced by church bells, cannon fire, and huzzahs. At a party that evening, N. B. Buford, a longtime Rock Island resident and member of the railroad's board, raised his glass to toast the "espousal . . . of the Mississippi River and the Atlantic Ocean." Less than 25 years had passed, he noted, since the first locomotive had run on American rails and less than two since rails had reached Chicago. Then citizens bundled against the cold to watch fireworks displays on both sides of the river. A larger celebration of the new railroad would wait for warmer weather.

On the morning of June 5, two special trains packed with Rock Island stockholders, investors, journalists, politicians, and distinguished guests (among them former President Millard Fillmore) rolled out of Chicago for the formal opening of the 181-mile line. In the evening there was the usual grand banquet with speeches and toasts, and the next day guests boarded five chartered steamboats for two days of excursions along the river. Among their destinations was St. Paul, Minnesota, where citizens were already talking about a railroad of their own.

In August, a full year and a half before the promised date, Farnam and Sheffield officially turned over the Chicago & Rock Island to its directors. Some track still awaited ballast, and a couple stations had not been finished; however, it was already a working, profitable business. In fact, more engines and cars were needed to handle traffic. Directors voted the necessary funds and elected Henry Farnam president. Farnam's financial associate, Joseph Sheffield, 61, wanted to devote his remaining years to philanthropy. One of his last official acts was to arrange for a first-day excursion train on the Peoria & Bureau Valley, now leased to the Rock Island. In November, he retired. To take his place, Farnam chose the energetic and ambitious Thomas Durant.

Beyond the end of track rolled the waters of the Mississippi, and plans were already in place to cross them. A group of the road's directors had obtained a charter from the legislature for the Railroad Bridge Company. Farnam was president and chief engineer, and its bonds were guaranteed by the Chicago & Rock Island and the Mississippi & Missouri railroads. The new company would construct the Illinois side of the bridge to mid-channel; M&M would build the Iowa side, with the ever-helpful Antoine LeClair donating the needed land. Construction would occur in three segments: a short span across The Slough, right-of-way across Rock Island, and the main section. The wooden Howe truss superstructure would march across the river to Davenport on six granite piers, the

The eastbound local behind GP7 No. 4517 makes its leisurely way along the banks of the Illinois River at Peru on June 8, 1975. The river, the railroad, and the nearby Illinois and Michigan Canal once made this a thriving port. *Bill Marvel*

Abe Lincoln for the Defense

The wreck of the *Effie Afton* in the darkness of May 6, 1856, had consequences far beyond the destruction of a boat and damage to a bridge.

The boat, valued at $50,000, was a complete loss. Of the cattle she carried, a few found their way to shore—the rest were swept downstream by the brisk current. Fortunately, all passengers escaped before fire, caused by the embers from an overturned stove, swept the superstructure. As for the railroad bridge the boat hit, the fire destroyed one span and the impact of the boat damaged the pier. It would remain closed four months for repairs. Passengers from the two daily passenger trains and the contents of hundreds of freight cars would have to be ferried across the river.

After the incident, folks in Rock Island and Davenport wondered what the *Effie Afton* was even doing on the river. She was an Ohio River boat, her usual run was between New Orleans and Louisville. This was her first trip on the upper Mississippi, and she was running after dark, a time when many steamboats tied up. There were rumors that she had been packed with combustibles and deliberately rammed into the pier by her captain, John Hurd.

Hurd, who was also the boat's part-owner, filed suit in U.S. Circuit Court in Chicago, the Honorable John McLean presiding. He asked damages and that the court order the bridge demolished as a menace to navigation and a public nuisance.

The case was crucial, and Rock Island's president, Henry Farnam, wanted the best legal talent he could find. "There is only one man in this country who can take this case and win it," said Norman B. Judd, the road's general counsel. "And that is Abraham Lincoln."

As a member of the Whig Party, Lincoln had voted in favor of pro-railroad legislation. "No other improvement," he had said during an 1832 speech, "can equal the utility of the railroad." In 1849 he had returned to Illinois after a single term in the U.S. Congress and built up a lucrative law practice representing railroads. In a celebrated 1854 case, he managed to get Illinois Central exempted from county property taxes.

Lincoln approached *Hurd et al. vs. Railroad Bridge Co.* with his customary thoroughness and imagination.

Illinois attorney Abraham Lincoln. *Library of Congress Prints and Photographs Division*

He studied survey charts of the river prepared earlier by a young army officer named Robert E. Lee. Then he visited the site of the wreck, sitting on a bridge stringer with a local 12-year-old boy, dropping a weighted string into the water to measure the current.

As the railroad's lead counsel, Lincoln delivered the final argument in the Chicago courtroom on Tuesday, September 22, 1857. The evidence, he said, clearly established that the wreck could not have happened as Captain Hurd had testified. Either Hurd had been careless and negligent, or the boat had been defective. As to the bridge obstructing navigation, Lincoln told the jury, the railroad operated year-round while river traffic halted in winter. If the Republic was to thrive, commerce, which flowed as much east to west as north to south, would depend on railroads.

The jury was unable to decide, and before the case could be retried, the plaintiffs dropped their suit. There were further legal challenges to the bridge by steamboat interests, one of them finally finding its way to the U.S. Supreme Court, where justices in 1862 found for the railroad and the bridge. The principle enunciated by Abraham Lincoln in that Chicago courtroom six years before was affirmed: The railroad has as good a right to cross a river as a steamboat has to sail upon its waters.

Above: One oddity Rock Island didn't buy: No. 920, a standard Fiat Model 668.920 railcar, demonstrated on the suburban district in summer and fall 1977. The hope was that the "Ravioli Rocket," as it was dubbed, would cut expenses on off-time suburban runs. Apparently, it didn't. *Author collection*

Overleaf: Coming up Fifth Street in Davenport, Iowa, on July 1, 1978, Silvis-rebuild GP7 No. 4515 leads another Silvis grad, a Conrail geep, on a shakedown run, westward toward Council Bluffs. The crossover in the foreground leads to the Kansas City line at the Missouri Division junction. *John Dziobko*

largest anchoring a pivoting center span on the Illinois side.

In September 1854, the cornerstone was set in place in Davenport.

Almost immediately there was an outcry from steamboat interests along the river who protested that the bridge would interfere with navigation. U.S. Secretary of War Jefferson Davis also opposed the bridge, for his own reasons. Its completion, he realized, would give impetus to a proposed northern transcontinental railroad route, isolating the South. Davis pressed the U.S. attorney for southern Illinois to file for an injunction, and in July 1855, the case of *United States v. Bridge Company et al.* came before U.S. Circuit Court. There John McLean, assistant justice of the Supreme Court, decided in the bridge's favor. Within nine months, the work was finished. On April 21, 1856, as Henry Farnam watched from the shore, Rock Island

locomotive *Fort Des Moines* rolled across the 1,528-foot-long structure and into the Davenport depot. Two days later, to the sound of clanging church bells, regular service began between Rock Island and Davenport. Seven other railroads had reached the Mississippi, but only Rock Island had crossed it.

The steamboat interests did not surrender. On May 6, two weeks after the bridge opened to traffic, the steamboat *Effie Afton*, bound for St. Paul out of St. Louis with passengers, *continued on page 26*

continued from page 23

lumber, and livestock, passed upstream through the draw. The current was strong, and she had made only about 200 feet when a paddlewheel failed. Adrift, the boat fishtailed to starboard, slipped back, slammed into a pier, and caught fire. Flames destroyed the boat and one of the bridge's spans. Owners of the *Effie Afton* promptly filed suit for damages, but loss of the steamboat wasn't the issue. Damage to the steamboat interests was, and the suit's ultimate objective was the removal of the bridge and the competition it represented.

The dispute labored through the courts for six years—in the early stages the Rock Island was represented by a promising young attorney, Abraham Lincoln—until 1862, when the U.S. Supreme Court found for the railroad and the bridge. The decision effectively represented the end of the steamboat era. Henceforth rails, not water, would carry the nation's commerce. (Repaired in five months, the original wooden structure succumbed to age in 1866 and was replaced by a second wooden bridge. When that bridge was damaged by a tornado, a third bridge, this one constructed of iron, was built on a new alignment. Today, a fourth bridge spans the river.)

M&M: Beyond the River

Although traffic crossed the river—12,586 freight cars and 74,179 passengers by August 1857—it didn't move much beyond it.

The Mississippi & Missouri Railroad had made slow progress since June 1855, when the first spikes were hammered down on the line west toward Iowa City. The first locomotive, the *Antoine LeClair*, had arrived and pulled an excursion 12 miles to the end of track at Walcott. Then 13 miles beyond, at Wilton, track gangs veered south toward Muscatine. That town had been clamoring for a railroad, and it had Thomas Durant's ear. Iowa City and Council Bluffs would have to wait.

The first train slogged into Muscatine in mud and driving rain on November 20. To get

railroad moving their way again, citizens of Iowa City raised a $50,000 cash bonus, to be paid M&M provided a train arrive before the end of the year. At Christmas, work gangs were still about 2 1/2 miles short, laboring to lay track across the frozen ground. Townspeople hurried out to help them. On the last day of December, temporary tracks were laid to the station, but the engine froze to the rails a scant 200 yards away. Workers and bystanders descended on the stalled locomotive and, with the minutes ticking away, managed to manhandle it the final yards. It was reported that the engineer collapsed beside his engine, either from exhaustion or hypothermia. The temperature was 18 degrees below 0.

With the nation sliding into a recession, there would be no further construction for several years. Over the next year and a half, more than 5,000 businesses would fail. Prospects were bleak for completion of the line, Farnam wrote to a New York associate. He was out of money and hoped only to salvage enough for "my dear wife and family."

The Land Grant Act, passed by Congress in May 1856, helped some. It assigned to states certain public lands that could then be passed on to railroads for sale or settlement. But with the M&M dead in its tracks at Iowa City, that state's citizens were not feeling very generous. Those to the west still waiting for rail service demanded that the state withdraw M&M's charter. In 1858 construction crews managed to push the Muscatine Branch 27 miles to Washington. But it would be 1862 before the main line from Iowa City would creep into Grinnell, 66 miles west. There was a war on.

As rails reached Grinnell, President Abraham Lincoln signed the first Pacific Railroad Act, setting Council Bluffs as the eastern terminus of the proposed transcontinental railroad. Four railroads were already racing across Iowa toward the Missouri River. M&M seemed to be in position to reach it first. Still, its rails did not move.

The Keokuk, Fort Des Moines & Minnesota Rail Road had been building northwestward up the Des Moines River Valley since 1853. Reincorporated as the Des Moines Valley Railroad, it reached its namesake city, now the state capital, in August 1866, causing the M&M to forfeit the $10,000 bonus the city had offered for an early arrival.

Loss of the bonus was the least of M&M's problems. A month before, the now-bankrupt railroad had been sold in foreclosure on the steps of the Davenport courthouse. In one of those complications that only a lawyer could love, the buyers had incorporated themselves as the Chicago, Rock Island & Pacific Railroad

Daisies are blooming along the right-of-way in July 1978, as U33B No. 290, temporarily separated from its usual companion, road slug No. 282, brings an eastbound through Oak Forest just outside of Chicago. *Terry Norton*

("Pacific No. 1," for legal purposes). Shortly thereafter, Pacific No. 1 was consolidated with Pacific No. 2, the Chicago, Rock Island & Pacific Railroad, and the modern Chicago, Rock Island & Pacific was born.

Back in Illinois, the Rock Island prospered. The road was hauling as much traffic eastbound as westbound, a sign that its territory was settled and producing goods as well as consuming them. Gross income rose from $1.2 million in its first full year of

Fort Worth's busy Tower 55 presides over passage of a transfer for Southern Pacific behind a dog's-breakfast assortment of motive power in October 1978. A smoky U30C No. 4596 leads GP7 No. 1267, GP9 No. 1331, and SW1200 No. 930. *Ed Seay Jr.*

operation to $1.5 million in 1863. Farnam took the opportunity to step down. Charles W. Durant took his place, and in 1866, John F. Tracy replaced Durant.

Tracy, a bachelor married only to the railroad, guided the Rock Island for the next 11 years, with a steady hand on the throttle and a keen eye on the track ahead, according to Frank P. Donovan in his collection of essays, *Iowa Railroads*. The new president got construction moving forward again, pushing the line into Des Moines, where it was greeted with less than enthusiasm. Though

harried by a flock of shareholder lawsuits challenging purchase of the M&M (Tracy was briefly arrested), he lobbied the Iowa legislature, persuading lawmakers to recognize the consolidation, allow Rock Island to keep M&M's land grants, and set a date of June 1, 1869, for completion of the road to Council Bluffs. Failing that, Rock Island would forfeit all further claims to land grants.

The road beat the deadline by 19 days. But its May 10 arrival in Council Bluffs was anticlimactic. Just one day before and some 1,090 miles west on a windswept sage flat near Promontory, Utah, the last rail was laid and the last spike driven, uniting the Union Pacific and the Central Pacific railroads and bridging the nation with rails from coast to coast.

Furthermore, the Cedar Rapids & Missouri River Railroad—a component of Rock Island's perpetual nemesis, Chicago & North Western—had pulled into Council Bluffs more than two years before, in January 1867. It was followed in August 1868 by the Council Bluffs & St. Joseph. Both received the lion's share of Union Pacific traffic. It was an omen of things to come.

John Tracy tried to make the best of the situation. In 1867, Grant Locomotive Works of Paterson, New Jersey, had built an engine for display at the 1869 Paris Exposition. Clad in burnished German silver from smokestack to boiler and from cylinders to domes, it was named *America*, and the

gleaming 4-4-0 had won the exposition's grand prix, or gold medal. When it was shipped back to the States, Rock Island's chief purchasing agent suggested to Tracy that the railroad buy it. It was placed on display at the railroad's new station at Van Buren and La Salle streets in Chicago. On May 15, 1869, coupled to four other engines and a long string of coaches, *America* steamed into Council Bluffs' Pearl Street station, an elegant, if belated, tribute to the nation's first transcontinental railroad.

It's May 4, 1980, and what began almost exactly 111 years ago when Rock Island rails arrived at the banks of the Missouri River is ending as GP38-2 No. 4355 leads the last train out of Council Bluffs. The units arrived the day before, returning a string of GP40s and U28Bs to owner Union Pacific. *Jim Rasmussen*

One of only 28 C-C units on Rock Island, U30C No. 4592 was purchased for grain trains, but in April 1975, it leads piggybacks on the Golden State Route east of Columbus Junction, Iowa. *Terry Norton*

CHAPTER TWO

A BEND IN THE ROAD

Rock Island's late arrival in Council Bluffs left it with a dilemma: Which way to turn? The way west was blocked by Union Pacific. Iowa was fertile ground for branch lines. Minnesota still beckoned from the north. To the south laid Missouri, Kansas, Indian Territory, and Texas. Which way to turn?

All of the above, it turned out.

Since the end of the Civil War, U.S. railroad mileage had grown from 36,827 to 53,399. Before the war, railroads had grown by laying track into virgin territory. Now more and more, they secured and expanded territory by gobbling up other railroads. In 1871 John Tracy cast

a covetous eye on Chicago's first railroad, the Chicago & North Western, whose line laid parallel to and north of Rock Island's across Illinois and Iowa.

Tracy assigned the task of acquiring North Western to another one of those bright and ambitious young men of which New England seemed to have an unlimited supply. Henry H. Porter was only 15 when he arrived in Chicago from Maine. When Henry Farnham was laying track across Illinois, Porter was already a $400-a-year clerk for the Galena & Chicago Union, Chicago & North Western's predecessor. In 1867, as Rock Island struggled across Iowa toward Council Bluffs, Porter became a director of

The scene down by the Caldwell, Kansas, train station is deceptively peaceful in this picture made by local photographer W. O. Armantrout. But the town, on the Chisholm Trail down by the Indian Territory border, had a reputation for general hell-raising, and in the 1890s, when this photograph was made, it was the jumping-off point for the frantic Oklahoma Land Rush. *W. O. Armantrout photo, courtesy Denver Public Library, Western History Collection*

the First National Bank of Chicago. He knew who owned stock in what, who was buying, and who was selling. A month after the first Rock Island train rolled to the banks of the Missouri River, Porter was named a Rock Island director. The following year, Tracy, Porter, and several others on the Rock Island board were elected to the North Western's board, and Tracy became North Western's president. He left it to Porter to work out details of a Rock Island–North Western merger. Then he turned to other matters.

Completion of the Transcontinental Railroad led to a three-way battle for eastbound traffic out of Omaha. The Chicago,

Burlington & Quincy, or simply the Burlington, whose line paralleled Rock Island's to the south, had southern Iowa sewn up. North Western owned the north. In the summer of 1870, after consulting with North Western's board, Tracy proposed that rather than compete, the three roads divide the spoils. Half of all revenue from eastbound traffic would be shared equally. Prevailing rates would be sustained. Each road would agree not to build branches into the others' territories. No papers were signed, no agreements drawn up, no press releases sent out. The "Iowa Pool" agreement was done on a handshake and a wink, perhaps over cigars and brandy in some paneled board room or luxurious private car.

With competition under control, two of the three major rail links between Chicago and the western gateway were within John Tracy's grasp. He now looked southwest, where promoters in Leavenworth, Kansas, were pushing

Surely one of the most beautiful stations served by Rock Island was Rio Grande's Colorado Springs depot. In 1893, about the time this photo was made, poet Katharine Lee Bates stepped off the train here, checked into the adjacent Antlers Hotel, journeyed to the top of the Pikes Peak, and was inspired to write "America the Beautiful." The 1877-built facility stands today, home to a spaghetti restaurant. *Horace S. Poley photo, courtesy Denver Public Library, Western History Collection*

a railroad eastward from the Missouri River. They were about to build a bridge.

Since 1869, Tracy had had been building his own line across southern Iowa in the direction of Leavenworth. Underwritten by Rock Island, construction of the Chicago & Southwestern Railway made rapid progress from Washington, Iowa, to the Missouri border at Lineville. In late September 1871, the road arrived at Stillings Junction on the east bank of the river. Once again, roundhouse forces polished up the silver *America* and dispatched it on the celebratory excursion. General and Mrs. Ulysses S. Grant and Grant's onetime adversary, Confederate General P. G. T. Beauregard, climbed aboard—one wonders what they talked about as the miles rolled by. At Leavenworth, the party crossed the river by ferry, and after the usual festivities, the group traveled upriver to Council Bluffs and then returned to Chicago. By

spring, the iron bridge to Leavenworth was open for business. Beyond were Kansas and the great Southwest.

But it would be 10 years before Rock Island laid a single rail beyond Leavenworth.

The railroad was still celebrating its new opening to the West when catastrophe struck at its eastern end. In October 1871, Chicago was a city of closely packed frame houses, plank sidewalks, and narrow four- and five-story buildings. And it was suffering through a long dry spell. For weeks, members of the city's 185-man fire department had been called out every day to put out a blaze somewhere. On

THE GOVERNMENT BRIDGE BETWEEN DAVENPORT, IOWA AND ROCK ISLAND, ILL.

The fourth and final bridge to carry Rock Island trains across the Mississippi at Davenport was completed in 1896 and rested on the piers of the third, also known as Government Bridge. Widened for double track, it also accommodated, on a lower deck, foot traffic, automobiles, horse-drawn trolleys, and, until 1940, electric streetcars. *Author collection*

Saturday, October 7, they were summoned again, this time to Van Buren and South Clinton, where flames were advancing across a four-block neighborhood of lumber mills and coal yards just across the Chicago River from Rock Island's handsome new station and 400-foot train shed. Seventeen hours would pass before weary firefighters returned to their stations.

The next evening, Sunday, flames again licked up, this time on the Rock Island's side of the river, near the Loop. In less than an hour, winds pushed the fire north through shacks and shanties into the warehouse district. Whirlwinds of flame coiled into the air, scattering sparks everywhere. Rock Island's new station and train shed, freight depot, and general offices vanished in a storm of smoke and embers. Cashier Warren Purdy managed to shove many of the company's documents into the vault before running for his life. As it was, all maps and surveys were lost. Three sleepers, eight coaches, five head-end cars, and a half-dozen freight cars were burned down to their wheels. For two days and nights, the Great Chicago Fire raged on,

jumping the river and consuming most of the business district all the way to Lake Michigan before sputtering out in the first real rain in months. The city lay in smoking ruins. More than 17,000 buildings had been destroyed, 150 lives lost. Rail traffic halted.

In spite of losses put at $300,000, Rock Island wasted no time drawing up blueprints for a new station and train shed that were built in eight months. Opening festivities went on for two days.

The board of directors had every reason to celebrate. Despite the fire, revenue for the fiscal year ending in March 1872 was $5.9 million; the following year, it topped $6.4 million. Theirs was a very prosperous business.

Rock Island's president John Tracy, however, was struggling. He had plunged into the stock market and was losing heavily. The hoped-for merger with the North Western was unraveling. That road's revenues were shrinking even as Rock Island's were growing. Henry Porter finally had to tell the old man that it was no use. Aging and gaunt, Tracy relinquished presidency of the North Western on June 19, 1873. More and

more, he withdrew from Rock Island's affairs, delegating his duties to another shrewd New Englander, Hugh Riddle.

Riddle had been a New Hampshire schoolteacher before he went railroading on the Erie Railroad. Tracy had brought him over as general superintendent. Though prim and humorless, Riddle turned out to have a gift for public relations. He had organized the highly successful Leavenworth excursion. He was a tireless booster of line-side industries. As a reward, Tracy made him vice president.

One of Riddle's first duties was to make sense of the railroad's growing network of Iowa branches, affiliates, and acquisitions. The country's center was shifting westward, but Iowa was still not so far nor so long removed from the frontier. A reminder came on the evening of July 21, 1873, when Jesse and Frank James and their gang held up eastbound No. 2 as it climbed the grade toward the new settlement of Adair, Iowa. The take was small—not more than $4,000—but the robbery was a blow to the railroad's pride. Riddle dispatched extra trains full of special agents to the scene—in

Sometime after 1896, the noted scenic photographer William Henry Jackson set up his tripod on the bluffs above Rock Island, Illinois, and recorded this panorama. The railroad's roundhouse is on the banks of the Mississippi at right. In the distance is the fourth bridge, or Government Bridge. Courtesy Colorado Historical Society, Jackson Collection scan #20103781

vain, it turned out. After the incident, he hired security guards for certain trains and authorized engine crews to arm themselves. Armed guards could offer no protection against another kind of trouble on the horizon. On September 18, two months after the James Gang held up No. 2, the New York banking house of railroad financier Jay Cooke toppled, taking dozens of other banks down in a domino fashion and sucking air out of the economy. Railroads were America's largest industry, and they felt the effects earliest and longest. Everywhere traffic fell; track gangs and construction crews put down their tools and went home. In the next four years, one-fourth of the nation's 364 railroad companies rolled into bankruptcy.

Panic and Prosperity

The banking collapse of 1873 swept a number of smaller roads into Rock Island's lap. The

The Great Train Robbery

From their hiding places among the trees overlooking the cut, they could hear the engine laboring eastward up the grade from Turkey Creek. The sun had set now, a dim glow in the west. The first stars winked overhead.

Jesse was crouching in a narrow trench the gang had carved into the south embankment. He was fingering a rope that ran down to the roadbed and underneath the near rail. That afternoon the gang had broken into a section house and helped themselves to a crowbar and track tools. They had pried up a handful of spikes at the end of a rail section on the north side of the track—the outside of the curve—and removed the angle bars and bolts. The rope Jesse held was knotted through the bolt hole in the rail.

The orange glow of the engine's headlamp swept the distant brush as No. 2, the eastbound *Pacific Express*, bore down on the curve. Jesse waited . . . waited. Then he hauled back on the rope, hard.

Up in the cab, engineer Jack Rafferty saw the end of one of the rails on the track ahead suddenly snake out of alignment. By instinct, Rafferty slammed the throttle shut and yanked the airbrake valve. Airbrakes were a recent innovation—Rock Island had installed them only four years before. Fireman Denis Foley teetered on the deck, a shovel of coal poised at the firebox door. "Jack, what's the . . . ?"

The rocking 4-4-0 hit the ties, heeled over on its side, and skidded a few dozen yards. The tender upended, splintering the cab and burying Foley and, on top of him, Rafferty. The first baggage car, driven by the impact of

The outlaw Jesse James. *Library of Congress Prints and Photographs Division*

Des Moines Valley Railroad, chartered in 1853 to build a line from Keokuk to the Minnesota border, got as far as Fort Dodge before running out of cash. In 1873 the line was split, and in 1878 Riddle leased the part south of Des Moines. The Des Moines, Indianola & Missouri, a 21-mile branch built by Rock Island director B. F. Allen with money borrowed from the larger road, was broke by 1876 and vanished into Rock Island four years later. Meanwhile, the Rock was putting out tendrils into niches and corners of its growing empire. In 1874 it extended its line from Englewood south of Chicago to a steel mill and a lake harbor, fattening its traffic base. The Leavenworth line had already sprouted a branch toward Atchison, Kansas, where another bridge would be thrown across the Missouri and, farther east, from Washington to Knoxville. Other lines were groping from the baggage car behind it, rode up and over the tender. The rest of the seven cars remained on the rails.

There was a second's silence, then the pop-pop of revolvers and men shouting "Get away from that window!"

"Keep your goddamn heads down!"

And, "Open that safe or we'll blow your brains out!"

It was over in 10 minutes, and when the six or seven masked men galloped south into the darkness, they carried with them perhaps $4,000, far less than they had counted on. They left behind more than a ton of gold and silver bullion, too heavy to carry. The big $75,000 shipment of currency and securities that informants had nosed out in Council Bluffs had actually gone out on the previous night's train.

Contrary to early newspaper reports, nobody was shot. Rafferty died instantly of a broken neck. The fireman was bruised, but managed to crawl out of the wreckage, dragging the dead engineer with him. Assistant superintendent H. F. Royce from Council Bluffs, riding in the second baggage car that night, broke his nose when he was pitched forward by the crash. John Burgess, the express messenger, was scared witless when Jesse stuck his pistol right up under Burgess' nose and demanded the key to the safe. But the gang had not molested any passengers. "We're none of your petty thieves," they shouted from trackside. "We're robbing the rich for the poor."

"We're grangers," one of them added, as though that explained everything.

They were not grangers, of course—not robbing trains to protest high freight rates or railroad monopolies. Jesse and Frank James and the Younger brothers still bore a grudge for the fallen Confederacy. But mostly they were opportunists, outlaws, predators. For years they had been robbing banks all over the Midwest. Now they had turned their attention to trains.

What happened July 21, 1873, four miles west of Adair, Iowa, was not America's first train robbery, as sometimes reported. The Reno boys had begun holding up trains back in Indiana in the 1860s. The James brothers would go on to rob a half-dozen other trains, including, almost exactly eight years later, a Rock Island express near Winston, Missouri, on the Kansas City line.

But their encounter with No. 2 that sultry, mosquito-bit July evening made the James boys national legends, putting their names in newspaper headlines and their exploits—real or invented—in dime novels. The railroad and express company put a $5,000 price on their heads, though neither would ever be brought to justice for that crime. Rock Island hired armed guards, and engine crews and express messengers on certain trains were required to carry weapons.

The railroad cut, now smoothed over, is just a small park alongside County Road G-30. In 1954, Rock Island marked the site with a short length of track and a plaque, affixed to a drive wheel from one of its big 4-8-4s. That same year the railroad relocated 6.67 miles of its main line, including the climb up from Turkey Creek, a short distance to the south of the old grade.

Des Moines to Newton and to Indianola. Branches even had branches. Control of the Des Moines, Winterset & Southwestern gave Rock Island a line off the Indianola branch from Summerset to Winterset. It was all getting very complicated.

Rock Island had gambled on Leavenworth as the principal jumping-off point south of Omaha for points west. But in December 1879, the road hedged its bet and signed

an agreement with the Hannibal & St. Joseph Railroad for access to the burgeoning riverfront town then known as City of Kansas. A month later, its trains were sharing that city's union passenger depot with eight other roads. Kansas City was on its way to becoming one of the nation's great rail centers.

There was plenty of business for everyone. In 1875, five million passengers rode American trains; a decade later, twice

Above: In vogue around the turn of the century, Vauclain compounding proved a dead end. Engines used steam twice in over-and-under cylinders, but uneven piston forces created excessive wear on the crosshead. Here, Baldwin-built No. 1202 poses for a builder's type portrait at an unknown location, possibly for noted photographer William Henry Jackson. *Courtesy Colorado Historical Society, Jackson Collection scan #20101751*

Below: The line east from Denver is mostly downhill, but near Strasburg there's a short grade. Led by FA-1 No. 137, the five units on today's Train 82 are pouring it on this March afternoon in 1965. *Bill Marvel*

as many. However, those who boarded trains for the West still faced an ordeal. In the mid-1870s, passenger trains paused twice a day, noontime and evening, so passengers could dash for a station lunch counter and gulp a hurried meal. It was that or sandwiches and greasy boxes of cold fried chicken brought from home. A few roads in the East experimented with restaurant cars, but western roads resisted this expensive novelty. In 1881, Union Pacific, Burlington, and Santa Fe signed an agreement not to introduce dining service on Denver runs.

Where other roads saw costs and inconvenience, Hugh Riddle saw opportunity. While still vice president, he suggested to John Tracy that Rock Island look into onboard meal service. Tracy passed the recommendation along to general passenger agent A. M. Smith, and soon Rock Island ordered four restaurant cars to supplement its 15 luxury Palace cars. *Australia, Overland,*

In Rock Island's usual roundabout fashion, Train 82 has come out of Rio Grande's North Yard, Rock's home in Denver, and is making its way along Northwestern Terminal trackage toward Sandown Junction and Union Pacific's line east. Track in the foreground gives Rio Grande access to the Denver stockyards, no longer a busy place by September 1967. *Bill Marvel*

Oriental, and *Occidental* were painted forest green, decorated with hand-painted scrolls and cornucopias, and fitted with hanging brass lamps, carved benches, table linen, and fine china. The service, launched in 1877, was an almost immediate success. A commissary was established in Chicago to stock the icebox of westbound No. 1 with beef, fish, hams, and oysters. The road's first dining car steward, appropriately named Frank Stewart, arranged to purchase fresh eggs, butter, milk, and vegetables. Stewart's accounts, cash receipts, and the empty ice box were returned to Chicago on eastbound No. 2.

Western Bank Note and Engraving Company printed handsome menus advising passengers of the days' selections on "The Great Rock Island Route." A seven-course meal could be purchased for 75 cents. Employees paid half price. Fine wine and liquor were available by the bottle or flask, though not to on-duty trainmen.

The new decade, the 1880s, promised much, but only if Rock Island could get control of its sprawling corporate structure. Reorganization was long overdue, and on June 2, 1880, the railroad's attorneys filed

It's October 1968, and a GP7, GP9, and GP18, in order, are working their way through the River Bottoms on Kansas City Terminal tracks. They'll soon pass Union Station, Tower 3, cross over the Kansas River, and enter Armourdale Yard. *Paul Dolkos*

articles of consolidation with the Illinois secretary of state in Springfield. The next day, they filed papers in Iowa. This was more than a tidying up—this was a transformation of the Chicago, Rock Island & Pacific Railroad and its scattered properties into a whole new corporate structure: the Chicago, Rock Island & Pacific Rail*way*.

On the eve of consolidation, the road owned outright the original Chicago–Council Bluffs main line and the South Chicago branch to the lake; branches from Wilton, Iowa, to Washington and Oskaloosa and beyond to Knoxville, Iowa; the old Chicago & Southwestern line from Washington to Leavenworth, plus the Atchison branch;

Des Moines branches to Indianola and Winterset; the Newton & Monroe; the Atlantic Southern to Griswold; a line from Atlantic to Audubon, Iowa; and the Avoca, Macedonia & South Western from Avoca to Carson, Iowa.

Consolidation of the leased lines brought in the Peoria & Bureau Valley; the Keokuk–Des Moines line; trackage from the Missouri River bridge into Leavenworth; the Avoca, Harlan & Northern; the Guthrie & Northwestern from Menlo to Guthrie Center, Iowa; and the Keosauqua & Southwestern, from Keosauqua to Mount Zion, Iowa.

The following year, the road completed a line from Davenport to Muscatine.

All this was a necessary prelude to further expansion. In 1885 Rock Island acquired control of the 368-mile Burlington, Cedar Rapids & Northern, a road it had helped bail out of bankruptcy in 1876. This acquisition provided Rock Island the desired access to Minnesota and the Twin Cities, plus lines to Sioux Falls and Waterton, South Dakota. After halting at the Missouri River, Rock Island was on the move west again, too. Plans were already afoot to lay track beyond Leavenworth into Kansas, Colorado, Nebraska, and the Indian Territories of Oklahoma.

Only Union Pacific stood in its way.

In 1877 Jay Gould and Sidney Dillon had quietly begun buying Rock Island and Chicago & North Western stock with an eye to protecting their interests in Union Pacific. They were able to place representatives of both roads on Union Pacific's board, with the intention of renegotiating the Iowa Pool agreement in that road's favor. The two eastern roads also agreed not to lay track into UP's territory.

Train 73 has piggybacks and auto parts in tow as it makes its leisurely way across the little-remarked, seldom-photographed High Line at Manhattan, Kansas. Alas, this McFarland–Belleville line will not survive Rock Island's 1980 breakup. *Bill Marvel*

Hugh Riddle could see what was coming. At the June 6, 1883, annual meeting, he resigned the presidency. His place was taken by a Gould-Dillon pick, Ransom R. Cable.

A banking and real estate operator, Ransom Cable was the first nonrailroader to run the Rock Island. He had been elected to the board of directors in 1877, and it was immediately apparent that he had friends in very high places. Two years later, he was named to the newly created post of assistant to the president. With the 1880 consolidation, he became second vice president, in charge of operating and traffic. Unlike Riddle, who was an organizer and consolidator, Cable was a builder. Lest anyone wonder who was in charge, he added the designation "General Manager" to his title when he became president.

By then, the Iowa Pool was badly frayed. Each new railroad that arrived in Council Bluffs—Chicago Great Western, Wabash, Illinois Central—demanded a piece of the action. With arrival of the Milwaukee Road, Cable saw an opportunity and began negotiations with that road and UP to jointly develop and "protect" traffic over the three lines. Milwaukee and Rock Island would become, in effect, eastward extensions of UP. The so-called "Tripartite Pact" lasted less than a year. By then, the financial condition of UP had weakened. Never one to wait for

U28B No. 280 and F7A No. 127 bang across Missouri Pacific's double-track St. Louis line just east of Kansas City. In September 1971, Union Pacific control of MoPac is still a decade away, but the two roads regularly exchange motive power, which explains the UP units in the distance. *Paul Dolkos*

someone else, Cable decided that Rock Island would go it alone.

"The question of territorial rights no longer exists," he said. "Each road will build when and where it pleases." In 1886 Rock Island began laying track where it pleased—westward.

Across the Wide Missouri

The railroad was certainly prosperous enough to move forward on its own. Gross revenues for 1883, when Ransom Cable took office, were more than $12 million. A year later, he mortgaged the entire railroad to United

Overnight rain has left fields waterlogged near Iowa Falls on June 29, 1969, as steam-generator-equipped GP7 No. 1298 and GP40 No. 360 work a short freight east on the line to West Liberty, Iowa. The GP7 will lose its steam generator by the end of the year. *Bill Marvel*

States Trust Company of New York for funds needed to start construction.

The springboard for this westward leap would not be Leavenworth, but St. Joseph.

Rock Island's division solicitor in Trenton, Missouri—the man in charge of negotiating and buying up right-of-way—had been urging Cable to begin construction in Kansas as quickly as possible. Marcus Low was a man after Cable's own heart—a sharp legal mind with political connections and big ambitions. Cable had put Low in charge of Rock Island's subsidiary line from Altamont to St. Joseph, Missouri, and Low saw to it that the line's charter was amended to allow it to continue across the river into Kansas.

Now in command of the whole westward enterprise, Low hired a brilliant locating engineer, Hilon Parker, and moved his base of operations to Atchison, Kansas. In December 1886, he obtained a state charter for the Chicago, Kansas & Nebraska *Railway* to build and operate a railroad from northeastern Kansas to Wichita and also to Denver and Colorado Springs. The following March, Low chartered a Nebraska counterpart, the Chicago, Kansas & Nebraska *Railroad*. This charter included a line into Indian Territory

and beyond to Texas. The Kansas company then absorbed the Nebraska company.

Hilon Parker worked fast. His preliminary surveys of the route were finished even before the legislature in Topeka granted a charter. By summer 1886, dirt was flying. In autumn, track laying began.

The line march began at Elwood, Kansas, opposite St. Joseph. By winter, when the track gangs put down their shovels and mauls, the rails stretched 43 miles to Horton, a future shop town. By spring 1887, gangs were laying track into Topeka, the state capital. Low and Parker moved their headquarters there, and Low, whose mind was always hundreds of miles ahead of the track gangs, lobbied U.S. Congress for permission to build from southern Kansas across Indian Territory. In March he got the okay, including permission

Sheffield Interlocking on Kansas City's east side was one of those busy junctions where the visiting railfan could always count on a steady parade of trains. In January 1972, GP40 No. 372 is on Kansas City Terminal tracks, heading for Armourdale. *Paul Dolkos*

for a line all the way to the Gulf at Galveston and another to El Paso, gateway to Mexico. That summer, thanks to the shrewd generosity of a local landowner named Herington, the railroad established a future division point at Herington, Kansas, and rail gangs followed the old Chisholm Trail southward. Where cowboys had once driven cattle, track gangs now spiked down rail.

The northern portion of the line was also on the move. From Horton, crews swerved north into Nebraska before turning south again at Fairbury. Tracks arrived at Belleville, Kansas,

Hotshot No. 26 is about halfway along its Tucumcari–Memphis journey, near Holdenville in eastern Oklahoma, where Rock Island's Choctaw Route clings to the side of a bluff overlooking the Canadian River. On a bright January afternoon in 1972, No. 303 heads up an all-GP35 consist. The two blue boxcars are headed back home to the Louisville & Nashville. *Dale Jacobson*

in September. Shortly afterward, crews began building northwestward from McFarland on the Topeka line. In December 1887, the two lines met at Belleville, Kansas, and the following spring construction crews made a beeline across northern Kansas for Colorado. The first train rolled into Goodland on Independence Day 1888. Some 110 miles west, at Lake Sid-

ing—soon renamed Limon—grading crews had already crossed the old Kansas Pacific, now Union Pacific's Kansas City–Denver line. In November, rails reached Colorado Springs. For a brief period, Rock Island's trains gained access to Denver by way of the Rio Grande's former narrow gauge line along the foothills of the Rockies. Soon the railroad worked out an agreement with UP for trackage rights west of Limon. The Rock gained access to Pueblo and its growing steel industry via the Rio Grande and Santa Fe.

In the meantime, the railroad had also negotiated trackage rights over UP's Denver

In May 1973, the winter wheat harvest is underway in Oklahoma as a grain extra just south of Dover heads for the big elevators at Enid behind F9A No. 4167, an F9B, a U28A, and a GP35. The bay-window caboose is placed at the head of the train for convenience in switching elevators. *Dale Jacobson*

line between Kansas City and its own rails in Topeka. More and more, the original St. Joseph line was relegated to secondary status, as westbound traffic shifted to Kansas City, whose population was approaching 150,000.

In two years and four months, the Chicago, Kansas & Nebraska had spiked

GP7s Nos. 1209 and 1205 bring the northbound local through the gently rolling landscape south of Minco, Oklahoma, on the Fort Worth line. The weed-burner has recently passed this way in July 1973, carrying on the never-ending battle against trackside vegetation. *Dale Jacobson*

down more than 1,100 miles of track, some of the fastest railroad construction yet on the American continent, with more to come. It helped that the land was level for the most part. There were no great mountains to climb, no forests to clear, no large rivers to bridge. This was the Great Plains, once called the Great American Desert, but soon to become the nation's breadbasket.

Chicago, Kansas & Nebraska was doing more than its share to bring about this transformation. As early as 1856, the road's passenger department aggressively began promoting settlement of the western lands. Low fares and abundant land attracted immigrants from Eastern Europe, Germany, and Russia. Low himself traveled to Indian Territory to look over prospects. Then he went to Chicago to personally deliver the good news to Cable: Rock Island's future would sail

on a vast golden sea of wheat. Cable nodded his assent, and Low returned and began collecting good Kansas seed. In 1889 Rock Island's rails arrived at Hennessey on the southern edge of the Cherokee Strip. Within a few months, the daily southbound freight

was dropping off more than a dozen cars a day packed with household goods. A year of drought intervened, but as soon as the rains returned, Rock Island delivered 12 carloads of seed wheat to Hennessey. Any farmer could cart away 5 to 10 bushels at cost, no interest.

One of the heaviest and most powerful B-B units on the system, U33B No. 198 is doing the work of a lowly geep as it creeps eastbound through Nichols, Iowa. A lonely grain elevator, wobbly tracks, and a handful of cars—this is what the branch down to Burlington has come to by April 1975. *Terry Norton*

What could be more pleasant in the heat of a 1975 July evening than standing out in the yard by the garden and watching GP7 No. 4517 pull out of Burlington, Iowa, with the evening freight for Columbus Junction? Up front, GP7 No. 4517 is dressed in bright new blue and white, a fresh product of the Capital Rebuild Program at Silvis. *Dick Hovey*

By then, the railhead had moved on to El Reno, and it was no longer the Chicago, Kansas & Nebraska. In a complex legal transaction, the entire line was transferred to Rock Island as payment for $1,143,000 the larger road had advanced for construction. Rock Island also purchased the Colorado extension for $1 million. Midsummer 1891, Rock Island was operating almost 4,000 miles of railroad line in seven states, plus Indian Territory.

Only now it was Oklahoma Territory. In 1890, Congress declared everything west of the Rock Island's line open to agricultural settlement. The "unassigned lands," some 1.9 million acres, opened literally with a bang at noon on April 22, 1889, when, at a gunshot, some 50,000 settlers in wagons, on horseback, even astride primitive bicycles, raced for 11,797 available homesteads in the new territory. They found some already occupied by "Sooners," those who had jumped the gun. Before the end of the day, two brand-new cities had sprung from virgin prairie: Enid and Oklahoma City, both with populations estimated at 10,000.

Rock Island had done its part by transporting many would-be settlers to the end of track at Pond Creek. The road stood to benefit even more on September 16, 1893, when the government threw open for settlement the Cherokee Strip south of the Kansas border. The mad rush of 1890 was repeated. The railroad attempted an end run around the rules by striking a deal with Cherokee elders under which members of the tribe would acquire land around projected Rock Island town sites in advance and later resell it to the railroad. The scheme misfired when the government declared that all new town sites be located 3 miles south of the railroad's depots. At Pound Creek and Enid, protests and even armed conflict erupted over which were the "real" town sites. The railroad refused to move its stations, and angry mobs tore up tracks, sawed through bridge timbers, and, in one case, moved an entire house into the path of an oncoming train.

Cable's troubles with Oklahoma settlers were easily solved compared to his problems with Union Pacific in Nebraska. Since 1887 he had been negotiating with that road for access to Omaha by way of the bridge from Council Bluffs. Rock Island's growing Denver and Colorado Springs traffic was following a winding, up-and-down route from Columbus

It's high summer 1977 as a matched quartet of year-old GP38-2s led by No. 4316—named *Garland L. Rucker* for the mayor of Herington, Kansas—swings across the Straight River at Owatonna, Minnesota, on Train 81. *Jim Rasmussen*

Bumped from commuter runs by Regional Transportation Authority F40PHs, all three of Rock Island's suburban F7As—Nos. 677, 675, and 676—break the stillness of a February 1978 snow in Pilcher Park as they work a westbound drag into Joliet. *Kevin Piper*

Junction, Iowa, through Trenton, Missouri, to St. Joseph. From there it passed through Horton, up to Fairbury, Nebraska, and back into Kansas. This was no way to run a railroad. Cable wanted to build right through Omaha to Fairbury, and to that end in 1889 he created the Iowa & Nebraska Railroad.

Union Pacific resisted. Cable pulled some strings, and the following year Congress authorized the new road to build its own competing bridge. When Milwaukee Road declared its intentions to use Rock Island's bridge, UP sat down to negotiate. The resulting agreement gave Rock Island rights on UP's bridge and on its line from Lincoln to Beatrice, Nebraska. In return, UP gained trackage rights over Rock Island from McPherson to Hutchison, Kansas. Rock Island immediately began work on its own line from South Omaha to Lincoln.

However, the agreement unraveled with a change in UP management that year. Now in control of UP, Jay Gould banished Rock Island from UP rails. UP thugs tore up all connections with Rock Island in Omaha, Lincoln, and Beatrice, and they derailed Milwaukee's locomotives and cars. Rock Island promptly filed suit in federal court and won.

The truth was, Rock Island was thriving, and UP was not.

Rock Island rails were moving steadily toward Texas, where the Chicago, Rock Island & Texas president—Marcus Low—was building north from Fort Worth. The new line west of Omaha was open. The railroad had elevated its trackage in the Chicago area and opened an alternative line from Gresham to Blue Island, where diminutive 2-6-6 suburban engines were already at work hauling commuters. By 1897

a rebuilt double-track bridge carried its trains across the Mississippi at its namesake city. The railroad's mileage had doubled and then some. Iron rails had been replaced by steel rails, wood-burning locomotives were giving way to coal-burners.

In 1898, Rock Island's gross revenues were just shy of an astonishing $20 million. Ransom Cable took the occasion to resign the presidency and become chairman of the board, Rock Island's first. Warren G. Purdy, the road's longtime second vice president, secretary, and treasurer, became president. Purdy started at Rock Island as a clerk and accountant, and he was the one who had saved much of the road's paperwork by locking it in the vault during the Great Chicago Fire.

A La Fayette, Illinois–Riverdale, Iowa, unit coal train catches the afternoon sunlight at Silvis behind a freshly painted GP9-F9B-F9B-F9B-GP9 combination. The train has come up the "other" Peoria line, via Galva and Coal Valley. Alas, Rock Island will not survive to catch the great coal rush of the 1990s. *John Dziobko*

Promoted from suburban service, E8A No. 661 hustles a trio of U-boats past Blue Island Crossing, one of Chicagoland's busiest, on Train 57, the hot daily service with auto parts for Los Angeles, in March 1978. *Kevin Piper*

In July 1915, No. 671 has come loping over the plains into Denver with a
local passenger run and now awaits an eastbound assignment on the ready
tracks at Rio Grande's Burnham engine house. The Rock Island–built 4-4-
0's 79-inch drivers provide speed, if the load is light. *Otto C. Perry photo,
courtesy Denver Public Library, Western History Collection*

CHAPTER THREE

A ROCKY ROAD

The great era of railroad-building was ending.

On July 12, 1893, historian Frederick Jackson Turner addressed a distinguished gathering of colleagues at the World Columbian Exposition in Chicago's Jackson Park. Many of those present had ridden Rock Island trains to the fair, where they could stroll the grounds and view the railroad's exhibit of the agricultural bounty being grown along its line.

Turner's paper had far-reaching implications for the road's future. In it, he declared that the western frontier, the possibilities it entailed, and the energies that it had called forth had made America unique among nations.

But that source of uniqueness, of greatness, Turner told the assembled historians, was at an end. The West was being settled. The frontier, he announced, was closed.

Within a few years, the Los Angeles & Salt Lake laid rails across Utah and Nevada toward southern California. David Moffat began his final assault on the Rockies with construction of the Denver, Northwestern & Pacific. In 1905 Milwaukee Road's directors approved extension of that line west to Seattle.

But at the start of the new century, it was hard to imagine where yet another transcontinental railroad would fit in. The "Pacific" in Rock Island's corporate title

The second Rock Island 2-8-0 in as many years, numbered 1799, poses on the turntable at Eddystone, Pennsylvania, in 1907. The first, an experimental engine Baldwin built and exhibited at the Jamestown, Virginia, Exposition in 1906, proved too heavy for Rock Island's track and was sold to New York, Susquehanna & Western. This replacement was too light, but nevertheless it survived to be renumbered 2200. *Author collection*

must have seemed an increasingly unlikely destination to those guiding the road's future.

The Rock had not yet reached its full extent. It still had territorial ambitions, but Cable preferred leasing lines to building new ones. And where he did build, he built on the cheap. Of the 3,568 miles operated in 1898, the Rock Island owned 2,877. The rest were leased or operated through trackage rights, for which the road was paying almost $800,000 a year. Not a wise use of the road's healthy surplus.

When Warren Purdy took office, he launched a long-overdue industrial development campaign. He set out to improve the physical plant, introducing the long-legged 4-4-2 Atlantic speedsters and heavy 2-8-0s in freight service. He put out branch lines probing for promising sources of traffic. The ring of mauls on spikes could be heard all across Oklahoma Territory, from Enid to Greenfield Junction, Geary to Anandarko, Anandarko to Fort Sill and Lawton. Purdy pushed the Guthrie & Kingfisher Railway

During a quiet moment between trains at Rock Island's "old" Peoria depot, a horse-drawn wagon unloads a boxcar along the Water Street team track. Built in 1891, the station lost its clock tower in 1939 and saw its last train in 1975, but it survived to be listed on the U.S. National Register of Historic Places in 1978. *Author collection*

Rock Island Shops and Round House, Goodland, Kansas.

Left: Goodland, Kansas, had been a town for less than a year when the first Rock Island train arrived July 4, 1888. The road quickly established a division point and built a depot, hotel, roundhouse, and shops. Denver and the Rockies lie about 116 miles beyond that far, flat horizon in this 1915-era postcard view. *Author collection*

Below: The hostler at Limon, Colorado, is up on the Vanderbilt tender, watering No. 2556 for a run. On April 21, 1919, the three-year-old 2-8-2 still looks like she just rolled off the erecting room floor at Baldwin. *Otto C. Perry photo, courtesy Denver Public Library, Western History Collection*

Pacific No. 809—a 1903 product of Alco's Brooks works and a machine of almost primitive simplicity (saturated steam, inside valve motion, inboard trailing truck)—simmers at Kansas City, Missouri, in October 1921. *Otto C. Perry photo, courtesy Denver Public Library, Western History Collection*

into the Oklahoma territorial capital at Guthrie. A branch from Enid was sent to tap the oilfields beyond Billings. After a 12-year hiatus, the board finally authorized construction from Liberal west toward El Paso. Allied companies were building up through Texas and across New Mexico. Rock Island was on the move again.

The cash surplus that underwrote this activity attracted covetous eyes. In 1901 newspapers reported that a syndicate was buying up large blocks of Rock Island stock.

It was a strange little cabal that now set out to capture the Rock Island railroad. Today, when names such as Huntington, Gould, and Harriman evoke images of titans with vast fortunes and even vaster

appetites, the "Big Four of the Prairie"—as *Fortune* magazine later dubbed them—seem somehow *smaller* than life, little men whose ambitions outdistanced their abilities.

William B. Leeds always wanted to run a railroad, ever since his days as a minor official on the Pennsylvania Railroad. He made a fortune in the tin can business and was known thereafter as the "Tin Plate King." Brothers "Judge" William H. and James Hobart Moore (you could always tell them apart—the "Judge" wore an elegant full-length fur coat) had put together National Biscuit Company and Diamond Match, went on to create a paper mill, dumped that to form American Sheet Steel, and sold that to U.S. Steel. They were restless and they had capital, and Purdy never saw them coming.

His first warning was at the June 5, 1901, annual meeting, when the road's talented vice president and general manager Hilon Parker

In 1898 Rock Island's new president, Warren Purdy, set out to acquire modern power. One result was a class of high-stepping Atlantics, an example of which, a 1901 Brooks-built 4-4-2 No. 1005, awaits assignment in the Topeka engine terminal on October 13, 1921. *Otto C. Perry photo, courtesy Denver Public Library, Western History Collection*

was dumped in favor of Leeds' boyhood friend and lifelong business associate, David G. Reid. Leeds himself took a director's seat and was named president.

By December, Warren Purdy resigned. Cable remained as chairman, but he was scarcely more than a figurehead. The Rock Island was firmly in the hands of the Reid–Moore syndicate.

Within months Reid–Moore men replaced all but two of Rock Island's directors. The syndicate quickly bought the 600-mile Choctaw, Oklahoma & Gulf, paying an inflated $23 million. That line had struggled out of Memphis, Tennessee, as far as Elk City, Oklahoma, before running out of steam and cash. Next the syndicate picked up the bankrupt St. Louis, Kansas City & Colorado, a onetime narrow gauge property with ambitions to link Missouri's two largest cities. Finally, the Burlington, Cedar Rapids

& Northern was integrated into the Rock Island system.

Out West, crews pushed the railhead from Liberal straight through Dalhart, Texas, and on to an important link with El Paso & Northeastern at Santa Rosa, New Mexico. On a bitterly cold February morning in 1902, the last spike was driven in what would remain Rock Island's only claim to the Pacific of its title. Management announced a $100 prize for the best name for the new train that would begin service to California in November. The winner: *Golden State Limited.*

By the end of the same year, the Choctaw Route arrived in Amarillo, Texas. Construction continued in fits and starts until 1910, when

12346. C. R. I. & P. Depot, Ottawa, Ill.

Long-limbed Atlantic No. 1040 gets the once-over from straw-hatted platform idlers at Ottawa, Illinois, in this 1920s-era postcard view. With four or five cars tied to its tail, the 4-4-2 has been clicking off most of the 84.5 miles since La Salle Street at a mile a minute. *Author collection*

Choctaw rails joined the Golden State Route just north of Tucumcari, New Mexico. Rock Island set up shop in Tucumcari and leased the Santa Rosa segment to the El Paso line. The road ran a few desultory surveys further west, but no right-of-way was graded, no track laid.

Pyramid Scheme

It was not for lack of transcontinental ambitions. The Reid–Moore syndicate envisioned a railroad empire stretching from coast to coast and encompassing Lehigh Valley, Lake Erie & Western, Chicago & Alton, Saint Louis–San Francisco (the Frisco), and Southern Pacific. To realize this vision, the group would tap Rock Island's substantial earning power. In 1902 it created two companies on paper—Rock Island Company of New Jersey and Chicago, Rock Island & Pacific Railroad Company of Iowa—and set about acquiring all outstanding Rock Island stock. What followed was one of the most complex, outrageous, and—in the end—destructive financial schemes in American railroad history.

In exchange for each share of Rock Island common stock, the syndicate offered stockholders one share of common stock and one share of preferred stock in the New Jersey company, plus $100 in collateral bonds in the Iowa company. The sole source of income for the two companies were dividends paid on the common stock held in trust. Amazingly, 95 percent of the railroad's stockholders went for the deal.

The syndicate next went after the Frisco, making stockholders in that road roughly the same offer. Frisco officers were installed on Rock Island's board. By 1903, the two holding

The cover of a 32-page booklet produced by Rock Island in spring 1928 touts the railroad's services to Colorado Springs and Denver. One caption inside admonishes parents, "In Colorado, young lungs expand, young muscles harden and young cheeks redden as nowhere else." *Author collection*

Brooks-built No. 812 waits at Mayetta, Kansas, on the original St. Joseph, Missouri–Topeka line, while milk cans are loaded, sometime in 1928. The spindly 4-6-2 has been modernized with a centered electric headlight, but it still sports inside valve motion and an inboard trailing truck. *Bob Andrews photo, Tom Klinger collection*

companies were negotiating for half of the capital stock in Southern Pacific's Texas lines.

Not done with its work, the syndicate created yet another entity, Rock Island Improvement Company, which would acquire ownership of the railroad's physical plant, including shops, terminals, yards, locomotives, and cars. In March 1904, stockholders approved a motion to raise Rock Island's bonded debt to $275 million, to go to the improvement company for acquisition of property and rolling stock.

At this point, Leeds, the Tin Plate King, dropped out of the syndicate and resigned the presidency because of failing health. His place was taken by former Frisco vice president and general manager Benjamin L. Winchell, who immediately embarked on an inspection tour of the railroad. He found it in less than satisfactory shape.

With construction of the Choctaw Route stumbling toward Tucumcari, Rock Island went on a buying spree, patching together a string of short lines in Arkansas and Louisiana with the aim of reaching New Orleans. The Kansas City–St. Louis line was completed, and in 1906 Winchell acquired half-interest in the Trinity & Brazos Valley from Burlington subsidiary Colorado & Southern. This gave Rock Island entry to Houston and Galveston from Dallas and Fort Worth.

The syndicate went on spending, issuing $10 million in Rock Island bonds in exchange for control of Chicago & Alton, which in turn controlled Chicago & Eastern Illinois.

The dwarf signal, foreground, gives the location: Kansas City Terminal trackage on a dreary April morning in 1965, as the *Twin Star Rocket* pulls in from Minneapolis–St. Paul behind E7A No. 637. The train is losing more than $1 million a year, and by September, Rock Island will ask the ICC for permission to pull the plug. Permission denied, the train will struggle on for four more years as the *Plainsman*. *Bill Marvel*

Rock Island's debt was growing faster than its earnings. In six years Frisco stock had not brought in a penny, and Rock was paying interest not only on the Iowa company's bonds, but on the Frisco bonds issued in exchange for that road's stock. Rock Island did not even own its own equipment, but it had to pay interest on equipment bonds. What the syndicate had created, as described in Stuart Daggett's 1908 classic, *Railroad Reorganization*, was a pyramid. Three

U25B No. 202 left Rock Island tracks behind at Santa Rosa, 45 miles ago, and is hustling freight No. 992 on Southern Pacific track south of Vaughn, New Mexico, on July 29, 1967. After the Rock's 1980 collapse, the entire Golden State Route passed into SP's eager hands. *Bill Marvel*

companies were piled on top of each other, "of which one was to operate the railroad, one was to hold the stock of the operating company, and one was to hold the stock of the company which held the stock of the operating company." This could not go on, and by 1909 the road was in trouble.

B. F. Yoakum, a member of Rock Island's board, offered to take the Frisco off the syndicate's hands for $10.8 million, but first it would have to come up with the $7.3 million necessary to retire short-term Frisco bonds. The money would come from—where else?—Rock Island's treasury. Winchell was asked to resign, and Henry V. Mudge, a Santa Fe Railway man, took his place.

Mudge inherited a road in need of attention. The world was at war. Though the United States was not yet involved, it was supplying arms, food, and raw materials to future allies France and Britain. Growing demands were being made on all railroads. Rock Island's mileage had almost doubled since the turn of the century, to 8,328 miles. However, almost half those miles were laid on bare dirt without benefit of ballast. In many *continued on page 66*

Overleaf: Out at the eastern end of the Choctaw Route, No. 356 makes its way through Memphis with No. 38, headed for Kentucky Street Yard in June 1972. The snow pilot, though hardly needed here, was original equipment on GP40s. *Mike Woodruff*

continued on page 66

Above: In December 1972, No. 31 has met its eastbound counterpart, Train 30, at Yukon, Oklahoma, and is on the move again at Banner, a crossroads and grain elevator just east of El Reno. Up front, F9A No. 4165—former UP No. 535—has a Rock Island shield and not much else to identify its new owner. *Dale Jacobson*

Right: Westbound Freight 73 rumbles across the Gascondy River bridge with 63 cars behind GP40 No. 344 on March 29, 1975. Though tunnels have been enlarged for auto carriers and other high cars, the twisty 300-mile St. Louis–Kansas City line sees few trains and fewer railfans. It will not survive the Rock's collapse. *Mark Nelson*

continued from page 63

places, trains rocked along on rail weighing 70 pounds per yard, behind aging and underpowered locomotives. Mudge set about shoring up bridges and track and buying larger locomotives. He leased the St. Paul & Kansas City Short Line, and by filling a 67-mile gap, that gave the Rock a direct route between these key Midwest cities.

Under the syndicate, debt had ballooned from $67 million to $288 million, annual interest from $3 million to $12 million. Labor costs were growing. For the first time in its 61-year history, the Rock was running in the red. In March 1914, the road missed a dividend. Shareholders in the Iowa and New Jersey companies appointed a committee to protect their interests. By autumn the committee had filed for foreclosure. The syndicate repeatedly put off the annual meeting, but a reckoning was coming. In February 1915, a federal court ordered the sale of $71 million in Rock Island common stock held by the Iowa company. The single bidder, a New York banker, got it for 10 cents on the dollar. Bondholders fared no better. Faced with the need to come up with $2.5 million in interest payments by April 1, the syndicate frantically searched for a way out. Reid resigned. Moore secretly induced a Rock Island creditor to sue the road, hoping to force it into receivership. Still in the dark, shareholders finally managed to call an annual meeting for April 12 on friendly turf, in Chicago. The wrangling went on for 10 hours, but at the end the remaining syndicate members were voted out.

Eight days later, a representative of the stockholders traveled to New York, looking

continued on page 71

With St. Louis only 45.9 miles away, the crew of GP40 No. 364 faces the morning sun at Labadie, Missouri, as Manifest 38 nears the end of an overnight run across the hilly Kansas City line. By June 1972, service on the 300-mile line is down to twice daily. *Mike Woodruff*

continued from page 66

for $6 million to keep the Rock rolling for a few months more. At the road's New York office, he was met by awkward silence, except for a chattering stock ticker. One look at the uncoiling tape told the story: The Rock Island had been placed in receivership. Henry Mudge and Jacob M. Dickinson, secretary of war under President William Howard Taft, were appointed receivers.

It took almost two years to dig a working railroad out from under the rubble. Not only had the Reid–Moore syndicate loaded a staggering burden of debt on the road, the group had cloaked its maneuvers behind a tangle of dummy corporations, secret payrolls, and other dodges. The Interstate Commerce Commission (ICC) began an investigation. Hauled before the commission to account for his looting of Rock Island, David Reid blandly informed commissioners that he had no idea how much he had made, since "I burn my books at the end of each month."

In the end, the ICC estimated that it cost the railroad $20 million just to create the pyramid of paper companies that bought and sold the Frisco and Alton. The syndicate had stripped the railroad of any real assets. Receiver Jacob Dickinson managed to retrieve Rock Island's equipment from the improvement company by paying $20,000 cash and exchanging notes. He then sued the syndicate to recover at least some of the looted funds. With creditors clamoring for dismemberment of the railroad and competitors waiting to snatch up the pieces, Dickinson bargained and somehow held things together. Stockholders voted a new $29 million stock issue, creditors agreed, and on June 24, 1917, like a snake shedding its skin, Rock Island crawled out of bankruptcy.

Rock at War

Control of the road now rested with the New York banking house of Hayden, Stone and Company, which had led the fight against

Freshly painted and scarcely a week out of the Morrison-Knudsen shop at Boise, Idaho, GP7 No. 4432 rolls 54 cars through Belle, Missouri, on the Kansas City–St. Louis line on April 6, 1975. This unit is one of 120 older Geeps shipped off for rebuilding between 1975 and 1977.
Mark Nelson

the syndicate. The road's new president was a Hayden pick, James E. Gorman, whom Henry Mudge had brought over from the Santa Fe. Gorman was a traffic man, a handshaking salesman with little practical knowledge of railroading. Two months before he assumed office, the United States declared war on Germany. Now all railroads were struggling to feed the growing war machine. To stay afloat in the flood of traffic, Rock Island bought 30 new locomotives. In March 1918, President Woodrow Wilson nationalized the railroads, creating the United States Railroad Administration (USRA) to oversee and operate the industry. The country was divided into three areas—North, South, and West—and Gorman was named federal manager of the Rock Island and adjoining roads. Charles Hayden, president of the banking house, took over presidency of the Rock Island, now a corporation without a railroad to run.

USRA, which was running the railroads, allocated 30 additional locomotives and 2,000 new freight cars to Rock Island, rolling stock the road neither wanted nor needed. But in the end it paid $6.8 million for the new equipment and found work for it.

Almost two years after the war ended in November 1918, the government finally returned the railroads to their corporate owners. What the owners got back was a physical plant worn ragged by wartime service and a payroll swollen by wartime wages. Still, harvests were good, and oil had been discovered on line in Texas and Oklahoma. October 10, 1922, was the 70th anniversary of that first train from Chicago to Joliet behind the *Rocket*. To mark the event, the road again dispatched a special train between the two cities. Employees planted 102 memorial trees along the right-of-way.

Once again, the condition of that right-of-way was a growing concern. The Rock Island had never enjoyed a robust physical plant. Neglected during government ownership, bridges and trackwork barely supported the

road's largest locomotives, and larger ones were on the way.

Relations among top managers were even shakier. By 1923 Louis C. Fritch, a Seaboard Air Line Railroad man brought in by Hayden in 1918, was running the railroad. Home-grown talent had either been run off or had quit in discouragement. Hayden himself had his hands full. Not only was he chairman of the executive committee, but he was sitting on the boards of 58 other corporations and was chairman of the finance committee of American Locomotive Works, a company experiencing some difficulty. Soon, Rock Island was buying dozens of new Alco locomotives.

The road also was buying up stock in a neighboring railroad. Since the days of the syndicate, it seems that Rock Island just could not keep its hands off the St. Louis–San Francisco. As in syndicate days, Frisco stock was almost worthless, but Rock acquired 183,000 shares and Frisco men once again began filling chairs on Rock Island's board.

None of this solved Rock Island's lingering problem, which was the condition of its roadbed. Fixing it was not about the money. Year after year through the late 1920s, earnings increased—from $137 million to $147 million—and with them dividends—from 5 to 6 to 7 percent. In November 1929, the stock market crashed, but Rock Island went right on paying inflated dividends and buying cars and locomotives it didn't need—from Alco, of course. The road negotiated an agreement to relocate the Choctaw line from downtown to the outskirts of Oklahoma City. New branches were put out to gather wheat in the Texas Panhandle. A new, more direct line was established from Trenton to Birmingham, Missouri. The board declared another dividend.

At the December 1930, meeting board members learned that the road had secretly acquired 25,000 more shares in Frisco, paying $70 for each $46 share. Funded debt was now approaching $400 million, annual

Rock Island's Kansas City–St. Louis line, on the northern edge of the Ozarks, was mostly rivers and ridges, which meant tunnels, otherwise a rarity on the system. On April 6, 1975, Morrison-Knudsen rebuild No. 4432, formerly GP7 No. 1202, exits 700-foot Tunnel 1 at Freeburg with Train 74 for St. Louis. *Mark Nelson*

interest payments $13.8 million. All along the line, weeds grew between the rails. Ties rotted. Sidings filled with bad-order cars that could not be moved. Many bridges could not support those shiny new locomotives. The golden wheatfields of the Southwest withered. Wages were cut and employees were laid off. Still, the road declared a dividend.

In late 1931 Rock Island borrowed $8.8 million to keep its wheels rolling. Within six months, it tried to borrow $10 million more, from the Reconstruction Finance Corporation (RFC), the government agency created to shore up failing banks, railroads, and other vital businesses. Within a few months, it was back for yet another $2.5 million. In May 1932, the RFC refused. A month later, for the second time in its 80-

The Fordyce, Arkansas, agent gives the daily local a once-over on the line down to Louisiana on May 15, 1977. In its final days, this remote portion of the railroad will be spun off as a quasi-separate operating entity, the Little Rock. *Terry Norton*

year life, the Rock derailed into bankruptcy. It was scarcely alone. Denver & Rio Grande, Cotton Belt, and Chicago & North Western also were insolvent.

While several large banking firms—including Hayden, Stone and Company—undertook the task of reorganizing Rock Island, the trustee committee set about finding new business. James Gorman, by now a Rock Island veteran, put his sales skills to work attracting new traffic to the line. Education trains carried the message

of modern farming and soil conservation practices to the hinterland. A public relations office opened. According to the 1933 annual report, "business appears to be improving."

However, improved business was not what Rock Island needed. A consulting firm hired to diagnose the road's ailments recommended sale of the Choctaw Route and portions of the old Burlington, Cedar Rapids & Northern—radical surgery Rock Island's management was unwilling to accept. A railroad that was decrepit a few years before was now approaching senility. Most of the road had been built to nineteenth-century standards, and on much of the road those standards remained. A study of Rock

Deep in the heart of Texas, GP38-2 No. 4342 is 30 miles out of Houston on the former Burlington–Rock Island on September 2, 1979. Once a railroad in its own right, B-RI was merged into the Rock Island and Forth Worth & Denver in 1965 to become the jointly operated Texas Division. With Rock Island's demise in seven months, the line will become Burlington Northern property. *George W. Hamlin*

Island conducted for Reconstruction Finance Corporation by John Barriger III revealed that Rock Island spent almost 15 percent more to move a ton of freight over its line than the parallel Santa Fe.

Gorman was a salesman, but The Rock needed a real railroader. In late 1935, bankruptcy trustees tapped Missouri Pacific's senior vice president, Edward M. Durham Jr., to become Rock's chief executive officer. A restless, dynamic man, he was out on the road within a month, quizzing employees and customers, poking his nose into forgotten corners of the railroad. Conditions and morale were so alarming that Durham went straight to New York to bargain with

the road's creditors, then reported to the trustees. Armed with their approval, he set out to overhaul Rock Island from top—management—to bottom—right-of-way.

The old Hayden gang had to go. Out was Hayden appointee Louis Fritch, who had been operating the system since the 1920s. To take his place, Durham hired John Dow Farrington, 45, general manager of Burlington subsidiary Fort Worth & Denver.

CHAPTER FOUR

PLANNED PROGRESS

The man who saved the Rock Island railroad was a square-jawed, flinty-eyed railroader's railroader, a slow-talker who chose his words carefully and meant every syllable of each.

John Dow Farrington despised incompetence. When he encountered it in an underling, he would fix the man in a gray, unblinking stare, a crocodilian smile would tug at the corners of his mouth, and he would begin a reaming-out the employee would never forget. Farrington understood every detail of the railroad. And he was a demon on track maintenance. So as he rode north out of Fort Worth in the office car Edward M. Durham Jr. had sent to fetch him to his new job, he learned what he was up against. Rock Island's line to El Reno—and almost everywhere else—was a bone-shaking ordeal.

The first thing Farrington did when he came on board as chief operating officer—at $25,000 a year, the equivalent of $382,000 today—was take to the rails for

In this photo taken for the February 25, 1946 issue of *Life* magazine, a diesel gleams in the background as two 150-ton cranes lower No. 5009 onto its drivers after reconditioning at Silvis, circa 1945. Note the candles positioned between the wheels. These were found to be the least-glaring form of illumination for this sort of close-quarters work. *Photos by Bernard Hoffman/Time & Life Pictures/Getty Images*

The Depression is still on, but John Farrington, the new chief operating officer, has slashed the schedule of the California Red Ball by 20 hours, meaning the No. 5019, waiting at Armourdale, Kansas, on January 6, 1935, will soon be called upon to run like the wind. *J. T. Boyd photo, Tom Klinger collection*

six months in a V-8 Ford sedan equipped with flanged wheels. Everyone ducked when they saw it coming down the track.

It might stop anywhere, and its master, in a business suit and snap-brim fedora, would step out for a look around. He would walk the track for a distance, kicking tie plates and spikes, his sharp eyes missing nothing. He scrambled under bridges and prowled through roundhouses and back shops, quizzing everyone he encountered. It was his practice to take division engineers and roadmasters along on these excursions. Woe be to the supervisor whose answers were hesitant or inexact.

In Manly, Iowa, Farrington watched as one of the road's big, competent 4-8-4 Northerns rolled in with a freight. Tonnage was cut, and two smaller engines took over for the run north. "Why?" he asked. He was

told that a 35-foot bridge on the line could not bear the weight of the larger locomotive. The bridge was jointly owned with Milwaukee and would require $1,700 to replace.

Rock Island rebuilt the bridge at its own expense.

In fact, long sections of track were so fragile that they could not accommodate the Northerns, many of which sat idle in terminals. The Rock Island's expensive fleet of 4-8-4s was not earning its keep. When Farrington began his tour, the road had deferred almost $5 million in maintenance in order to generate those generous dividends so beloved by stockholders. The line from Omaha to Colorado Springs was so bad, some considered abandoning it. The Des Moines–Omaha main line would then be reduced to secondary status.

All across the railroad, the mood of employees was abysmal. Factional wars divided the office staff. Farrington quickly reversed direction. He enunciated a new policy and a slogan to go with it: The

4-8-4s Aplenty

Rock Island's steam roster was scarcely one to quicken the heart of a locomotive buff. Its engines were never the most powerful, heaviest, or fastest in their class. None were on the cutting edge of steam technology. The road rostered some high-stepping Atlantic 4-4-2s, but then so did most passenger railroads at the time. Like neighbor Missouri Pacific and several other railroads, it dabbled in compound technology with a single three-cylinder 4-6-2 that was set aside after a few years. No action photographs of it exist, leading one to suspect this locomotive spent most of its time on the shop line awaiting attention. The Rock was one of the early roads to adopt the Mountain type, fielding a pair of 4-8-2s numbered 998 and 999 and dubbed the "Gold Dust Twins." Neither was exceptional, but they sired a long line of good dual-service engines. Most of Rock Island's locomotives were adequate to the job, and no more.

But in one respect Rock Island did excel: It rostered more 4-8-4 Northerns than any other U.S. railroad—a total of 85, in two classes. They were not the largest or most powerful 4-8-4s, but they were fine locomotives and played an important role in keeping traffic fluid at a time when the Rock was threatened with hardened arteries.

Steam archivist Lloyd Stagner told their story in an article in the March 1981 issue of *Trains* magazine.

In the late 1920s, Rock Island decided to rev up its freight schedules. Trains were creeping along at an average 12.3 miles an hour, scarcely adequate to hustle fruit and other perishables from California to eastern markets or to return empties for timely reloading. Its most powerful engines, a group of lumbering 2-10-2s, were restricted to 30 miles an hour. In 1928, the road beat most of its rivals to the punch, ordering a single 4-8-4 from Alco, which under Rock chairman Charles Hayden had become the house provider of motive power. Hayden was also on Alco's executive committee.

No. 5000 arrived early the following year. With its concealed piping and smooth boiler jacket, the engine bore a family resemblance to New York Central's sleek Alco-built 4-6-4 Hudsons. No. 5000 was put to work from Silvis to Kansas City, where its booster, high-capacity boiler and 69-inch drivers moved things along faster—and on less coal—than the 2-10-2s.

Nos. 5112 and 5110 await assignment at Silvis, Illinois, in the last days of steam, dispossessed by new GP7s. Twenty of the 5100 series 4-8-4s were stored awaiting the fall harvest rush, but operating vice president Downing Jenks managed to borrow FTs from his former employer, Great Northern. *Author collection*

Within two months, the road ordered two dozen more, displacing the 2-10-2s from Silvis–Kansas City service. One month after the 1929 stock market crash, the road ordered 40 more. Their weight and Rock Island's precarious bridges restricted them to Chicago–Tucumcari, Herington–El Reno, and Davenport–Allerton service. Most were later converted to oil burners. All eventually got 74-inch drivers, roller bearings, and other improvements. (One, No. 5040, even got a bright-red boiler jacket for service on the *Golden State Limited*.) Under John Farrington's massive rebuilding of Rock Island, the big engines extended their territory, running all the way into Denver, St. Paul, and occasionally Fort Worth. For years they dominated California fruit blocks, and they kept war traffic moving. They could run like the wind on passenger trains, occasionally rocketing down the 70-mile tangent from Guymon, Oklahoma, to Dalhart, Texas, at 90 miles an hour.

During the war, Rock Island returned to Alco for 20 more 4-8-4s. Aside from their good looks—connoisseurs consider them among the handsomest 4-8-4s ever built—they were afterthoughts. The railroad really wanted diesels but because of wartime shortages had to make do with steam. Veteran enginemen preferred the earlier engines, which steamed more freely and, because they had boosters, were less slippery starting up.

New or old class, none of the 4-8-4s were preserved.

Baggage/mail and coach in hand, Ten-Wheeler No. 1506 makes 35 miles per hour at Apache, Oklahoma, with Train 704, the daily Lawton branch accommodation, on July 23, 1936. *Otto C. Perry photo, courtesy Denver Public Library, Western History Collection*

Rock Island would be the road of "Planned Progress," emphasis on *planned*. One by one, the old guard was pensioned off, their places taken by young hotshots brought over from the Burlington system. Some $20 million eventually was spent on the road's foundation—new rail, new ties, fresh ballast. To pay for these necessary repairs, Farrington announced a railroad-wide scrap drive. La Salle Street ordered employees to scour every foot of the system for anything that was idle

or cast aside. If it could be reused, reuse it. If not, sell it for scrap. Thousands of obsolete freight cars were junked, old engines cut up, miles of underutilized branch line taken up. The European powers were already gearing up for war, and scrap prices in 1937 were high. With a fresh $4.5 million in its pocket, the road bought 112-pound rail and shored up more than 140 bridges.

More far-reaching yet was a sweeping series of line improvements. Over much of its territory, Rock Island rails still followed their original alignments, snaking along creeks, bending to avoid hills, following the lay of the land up hill and down dale. Under the

continued on page 85

Clattering around the back streets of Topeka in the late 1930s, 0-6-0 No. 284 goes about its business while its replacement, an SW fresh from EMC, rumbles in the background. One of the last products of Alco's Pittsburgh works in 1919, the 0-6-0 labored on into the early 1950s. *Frank Kelley photo, Tom Lee/ Tom Klinger collection*

Hustling along west of Dalhart in the Texas Panhandle, Mountain type No. 4001 easily hits 50 miles per hour with the 12 cars of Train 4, the westbound *Golden State Limited*, on April 16, 1937. The engine is one of the "Gold Dust Twins," a pair of pioneering 4-8-2s delivered as Nos. 998 and 999 by The Schenectady Locomotive Works in 1913 and renumbered in 1920. *Otto C. Perry photo, courtesy Denver Public Library, Western History Collection*

Diesel Oddities

If Rock Island's steam roster was bland, its diesel roster was bizarre. Salesmen must have loved Rock Island. The road sampled the work of eight builders, major and minor. Six "orphan" models that nobody else wanted found a home there. J. David Ingles captured the exotic flavor of Rock Island diesel power in "Christine and the Mongeese" in the December 1965 *Trains* magazine.

Burdened with lightly patronized branch lines, the road in 1925 sampled a 37-foot International railbus before turning to distillate-powered Electro-Motive Corporation "doodlebugs" and gas-powered chain-drive McKeen cars. Once they got the hang of internal combustion, shop forces in Horton, Kansas, set to work, gutting two 40-foot steel mail cars and, with technical assistance from EMC, installing pairs of six-cylinder Winton distillate engines in each. Rated at 550 horsepower, each could pull 25 freight cars at 37 miles an hour on level track. Soon the two were earning their keep on rural lines, replacing 4-4-0s and even 2-8-0s. Two years later, Horton shops turned out three slightly larger versions, powered by dual eight-cylinder 400-horsepower engines. One managed to drag 10 loaded cars, 11 empties, and a caboose up a 1 percent grade at 8 miles an hour. Impressed, the road ordered seven copies from EMC and St. Louis Car Company. Steady troopers, they outlasted steam, the last one going to scrap in 1963.

All that was prologue. Facing smoke-abatement measures at the La Salle Street station, in 1930 Rock Island bought a battery-powered boxcab. The 10000 was assembled at GE's Erie, Pennsylvania, works alongside two identical New York Central engines. A 300-horsepower six-cylinder Ingersoll-Rand diesel recharged the bank of batteries, which could churn out more tractive effort than the road's husky 0-8-0s.

In the late 1930s came the fleet of passenger diesels and switchers that powered John Farrington's "Planned Progress" campaign. Seven sleek EMC TAs arrived in 1937, models unique to Rock Island. With their 1,200-horsepower Winton engines, they ran like greyhounds—up to 110 miles per hour with three or four Budd streamlined cars. But as *Rocket* passenger trains grew in popularity and length, the road turned to EMD (formerly EMC) and Alco for more powerful passenger

units. The EMDs proved clearly superior, and in 1940 the road ordered five of that builder's 2,000-horsepower E6As. To go with them, EMD delivered a pair of flat-faced AB6 boosters with cabs, single diesels, and baggage compartments. Only Rock Island needed them. The westbound *Rocky Mountain Rocket* split in Limon, Colorado, with the lead unit taking one section into Denver and an AB6 taking the other to Colorado Springs.

Union rules allowed for one-man operation of small engines, and in 1939–1940 the railroad bought small batches of 44-ton switchers from Whitcomb and on-line builder Davenport Bessler. Then the road tried out a half-dozen smaller Davenport 30-tonners. Mechanically driven and woefully underpowered, they waddled around the yards, side-rods flailing

Far more practical were four 1000-horsepower Alco RS-1s delivered in 1941. Essentially lengthened switchers

with a long hood, cab, and short hood, they set the pattern for generations of road-switchers to come. Almost immediately the U.S. War Department drafted them into military service, and the War Production Board soon allocated 11 more to the Rock.

As the war ended, the floodgates of diesel production opened. Rock Island's engine terminals filled with many of the standard models other road were buying—E- and F-units, Alco FAs (soon re-engined by EMD), SWs, GPs, and eventually GE U-boats. Here and there, something strange appeared. Five BL2s— "Mongeese"—were not quite cab units, not quite road-switchers. Only the Rock and Boston & Maine used them in commuter service. The Rock also assigned Fairbanks-Morse road-switchers to suburban service, re-engining them with EMD prime movers. Almost everything strange ended up pulling commuters. Most memorable were three EMD LWT12 lightweight streamliners—Nos. 1, 2, and 3—that, when

built in the mid-1950s, were heralded as saviors of the railroad passenger business.

But mostly Rock Island loved odd switchers: a pair of boxy Lima-Hamiltons and a pair of even boxier Davenport 112-ton center cabs that were known around the Quad Cities, where they worked, as the "Piano Crates." The motive power department continued its eccentric ways well into 1960s with 10 off-center-cab Century 415s, one of Alco's last efforts in the locomotive business.

Add to this the panoply of Rock Island paint schemes, the rebuilds, the borrowed and leased units, and you have a railroad that was up to the end seldom prosperous but never dull.

Left: The boss is in town. Appearance of inspection sedan No. 564 in Colorado Springs in early May 1938 probably signals to the troops that the road's dynamic chief operating officer, John D. Farrington, is somewhere nearby, poking around and asking questions. They better have answers ready. *Otto C. Perry photo, courtesy Denver Public Library, Western History Collection*

Below: Assigned to service on Missouri-Kansas Division branch lines for most of its life, St. Louis Car Company No. 9008 idles at the Liberal, Kansas, station January 20, 1939, probably awaiting departure for Amarillo over the 153-mile line via Stinnett. *Otto C. Perry photo, courtesy Denver Public Library, Western History Collection*

continued from page 80

new program, the crooked was made straight, the rough ways smoothed. As one project was finished, the savings realized would underwrite the next. In the end, the Rock Island would be a whole new railroad.

To deal with slumping passenger revenues, Farrington announced that the road would acquire a fleet of streamlined diesel-powered trains and put them into direct competition with rivals Burlington and Union Pacific/ Chicago & North Western, which already had streamliners and enjoyed shorter, more direct routes. Despite a lack of enthusiasm among Rock Island's directors, in 1937 the road ordered six Winton-powered Electro-

Built originally for Missouri Division service, a couple of Rock Island's big Schenectady-built 2-10-2s, Nos. 3029 and 3016, slug it out east of Tucumcari, New Mexico, on February 25, 1940, with 81 cars from Southern Pacific. Most of the Rock's 35 2-10-2s ended up working out of Dalhart on the Tucumcari line. *Otto C. Perry photo, courtesy Denver Public Library, Western History Collection*

Motive passenger diesels and 20 stainless-steel Budd passenger cars for service on the first of the new trains, the Chicago–Peoria *Rocket*. At the same time, Rock Island bought 10 Electro-Motive diesel switchers, its first.

These purchases, and those that followed, paid handsome dividends.

By the end of 1937, gross revenue had risen to $82 million, a big improvement over the $66 million earned in 1934. However, the

Less than a year old on May 8, 1940, the Samson of the Cimarron, Rock Island's massive bridge southwest of Liberal, Kansas, dwarfs the 14 cars of the *Golden State Limited*, headed for Los Angeles behind 4-8-2 No. 4046. The 1,269-foot bridge and 8.42-mile line relocation here were the first major projects in John D. Farrington's campaign to remake the railroad. *Otto C. Perry photo, courtesy Denver Public Library, Western History Collection*

economy had suffered a brief recession, and by 1938, business was down. Nevertheless, Farrington's improvement machine pressed onward. He decreed a second scrap drive—this one raised $8 million, almost twice as much as the first—and poured the money into a locomotive- and car-rebuilding program and other projects. The largest engines were modernized. The *Des Moines Rocket* was placed in service, and plans for the grandest *Rocket* of them all, the Chicago–

Colorado *Rocky Mountain Rocket*, were on the drawing board—in spite of the condition of the Colorado Springs line.

Nevertheless, the track gangs were busy. The new system standard 112-pound rail was being spiked down; hundreds of miles of new block signals were lighted; 43 new diesels were at work. Down in Kansas, the winding, flood-prone Cimarron River Crossing, bottleneck of the 1,100-mile Golden State Route, was spanned by a high steel bridge, one of the marvels of modern railroad engineering. As the 4-8-4s extended their territory (they were rolling into Denver by 1940), freights grew longer and ran faster. All these measures were saving money, $7 million a year by the early 1940s. In 1941, revenue was $96 million. The deficit had been eliminated, and for the first time in 10 years, Rock Island was running in the black.

Still, the railroad remained bogged down in bankruptcy for almost eight more years. Trustees submitted new reorganization plans to the Interstate Commerce Commission (ICC), only to see them turned down when creditors balked. In 1940 the ICC put forth its own plan. The Rock Island would not be allowed to pay out any more of those generous dividends until it had built up a healthy cash reserve. Not surprisingly, shareholders objected.

So matters stood on December 7, 1941.

Rock Embattled

The day Japanese planes appeared over Pearl Harbor, the Rock Island was physically as sound as it had been in years. By 1942, line relocations already completed were saving the road tens of thousands of train-miles, countless labor hours, and precious fuel. Passenger revenues were recovering. The new streamliners were earning a handsome 55 percent on their investment, after costs

Gleaming in the morning sun, DL107 No. 623 is west of Watkins, Colorado, with the seven-car Denver-bound *Rocky Mountain Rocket* on May 11, 1941. All windows and stripes and fussy Art Deco details, the Otto Kuhler–styled Alcos lacked the smooth lines—and reliability—of their EMC competitors. *Otto C. Perry photo, courtesy Denver Public Library, Western History Collection*

No. 2653, one of the road's numerous 2-8-2s, labors up the grade east of Peyton, Colorado, with the 22 cars of the daily Limon–Colorado Springs local. On this sunny January 10, 1943, the High Plains are between blizzards. *Otto C. Perry photo, courtesy Denver Public Library, Western History Collection*

and taxes. And the road now had extra equipment to deal with the coming flood of wartime passenger traffic. In 1942, Edward Durham retired, and Farrington became chief executive officer.

World War II did not catch American railroads unprepared. Ten days after Pearl Harbor, an office was set up within the U.S. War Department—as the Department of Defense was then known—to coordinate all military railroad traffic. A branch office was established in Chicago. Rock Island had already created its own military department.

Rock Island's rails were humming with lend-lease shipments destined for Britain, France, Russia, and China. The Association of American Railroads suspended rules governing interchange of freight cars. The National Guard and the Reserves had been activated in 1940, depriving Rock Island of many valued workers. Soon, mobilization cut deep into the ranks as veteran railroaders were called to war. Retired employees returned to work, and women were hired as engine wipers, clerks, tower operators, and

Motorcar No. 9071 burbles along near the El Dorado, Arkansas, division point on the line south from Little Rock, with Train 31 for Winnfield in deepest Louisiana. In June 1946, No. 9071 and sister No. 9070 are more or less permanently assigned to this run. *Robert W. Richardson photo, courtesy Denver Public Library, Western History Collection*

even shop workers. In the Southwest, tens of thousands of Mexican workers crossed the border—legally—to work on the railroads.

Within sight of the U.S. coast, German submarines were sinking oil tankers. In response, long tank trains snaked between oilfields and refineries. In a single day, American railroads delivered more than 900,000 barrels to their destinations. As a major player in the Gulf oilfields, much of this traffic fell to Rock Island. The road's freight car loadings rose by 6 percent in 1942. By 1943 Rock Island was hauling more than twice the carloads it had in 1939. The average freight car rolled 63 miles in a day, a

considerable improvement over the 45 miles in 1939. Passenger trains took sidings so that trains of tanks, jeeps, ship components, arms, and men could pass.

Those passenger trains were running full to more-than-full. Day after day, the *Golden State* and *Californian* sold out. Military personnel had priority, and civilians often *continued on page 92*

These images appeared in a photoessay on the Rock published in the February 25, 1946 issue of *Life* magazine. **Left:** Rock Island repairman James Notrdes changes a wheel in the 51st Street Yard in Chicago, circa 1946. **Above:** With the flick of a switch, dispatcher A. H. Reinhart moves train from one track to another on the 24 miles of double track (mapped at the top of the panel) between Rock Island and Atkinson, Illinois. *Photos by Bernard Hoffman/Time & Life Pictures/Getty Images*

A perfect set of FTs, 70-70B-70A, still conjoined by drawbars rather than couplers, rolls west through Topeka, Kansas, in October 1946, one year after delivery. *Tom Lee photo, Tom Klinger collection*

continued from page 89
found themselves standing in vestibules or sitting on suitcases in the aisles. In 1943 Rock Island carried more than 15 million passengers, a threefold increase over 1939. Fortunately, the road had 15 new sets of streamlined equipment to help shoulder the load. Still, many of its passenger cars had been diverted to service on troop specials, called "main trains" because they held the main line while everything else took sidings. Baggage cars were converted into sleepers and troop kitchens. Every six minutes, American railroads dispatched a troop train. With dozens of military bases and flying fields along its southwestern lines, Rock Island was one busy railroad. The road assigned a

passenger department representative to escort each main train. Heaven help the escort whose train ran out of ice or drinking water in the Texas Panhandle.

Not everything ran smoothly. During the 1943 Christmas rush, five railroad unions threatened to shut down the national railroad system over wages. President Franklin Roosevelt offered to arbitrate, but three of the unions rejected his offer. On December 27, Roosevelt ordered the U.S. Army to take over and, if necessary, run the nation's railroads. Within three weeks, the unions gave in.

Tank cars were in short supply, and the road made do stacking steel drums of crude in boxcars. More gondolas were needed. Cars were run into the ground, patched, and repatched. All 65 of the 4-8-4s were modernized. Because steel and other resources were diverted to the war effort, new equipment was hard to come by, but in 1943

Rock Island at its finest. A switchman guides R67B No. 5111 through the Blue Island Yards on August 30, 1947. The one-year-old coal-burner is assigned to service east of Kansas City. *Charles Kerrigan photo, Tom Klinger collection*

Rock Island started buying 4-8-4s in 1928, and in October 1947, no U.S. railroad had more of them. Here No. 5044, one of the original R-67 class and one of 85 Northerns on the road's roster, gets its tank topped off in Council Bluffs, Iowa. *Tom Klinger collection*

Passenger service to and from the Mile-High City wasn't all *Rockets*. On January 3, 1948, Pacific No. 909, equipped with one of the road's whale-back tenders, storms out of Denver with mostly head-end cars and a single coach for Belleville, Kansas. *Bob Andrews photo, Tom Klinger collection*

the War Production Board (WPB) authorized Rock Island to buy 500 new boxcars, 10 new oil-burning 4-8-4s, and a dozen Electro-Motive FT cab-and-booster sets. The diesels were put to work from Chicago to Kansas City, and the Northerns from Kansas City to Dalhart. A year later, the WPB authorized 10 more 4-8-4s, these coal-fired for service east of Kansas City.

In 1944, *Fortune* magazine assessed the road's planned progress under John Farrington. "Rock Island Revived," an unsigned article, detailed the extensive improvements to the Rock and noted the road's robust health. However, financial analysts were skeptical about long-term prospects. Almost everywhere Rock Island went, the article pointed out, a competing road went there more directly. Rock's trains crept into Dallas, Omaha, Kansas City, the Twin Cities, Memphis, Oklahoma City, and Denver over somebody else's rails. Overall, the road was a patchwork, not an integrated point-to-point system like its competitors. Analysts pegged postwar earnings at no more than $150 million, little more than the road had earned in 1929.

In fact, in 1946 Rock Island grossed $160 million. The following year, gross earnings climbed to $178 million and kept on climbing. It was a leaner, meaner railroad. Fewer locomotives were doing more. Where traffic was dense, track gangs were replacing 112-pound with 131-pound rail. When Farrington took command, only 191 miles were under Centralized Traffic Control (CTC), and Automatic Block Signals (ABS) governed only 1,266 miles. Now 428 miles were under CTC and more than 2,000 miles under ABS.

For all that, the road was still slogging up the long grade out of bankruptcy. Trustee Frank Lowden had died. To replace him, the court appointed Chicago banker and real estate developer Aaron J. Colnon. Colnon was an ambitious man. When the Rock Island emerged from bankruptcy, he wanted to be in command, and he immediately set out to derail John Farrington. (Years later, Colnon's meddlesome nature entangled him in the fight over the remains of the Tucker motorcar company.)

continued on page 98

Rebuilding the Rock

The Rock Island of the 1930s was still very much the Rock Island of the 1880s. Much of the original route, laid out when straining 4-4-0s and wooden freight cars were the rule, was still in place. However, now the rails had to accommodate 2-8-2s, 4-8-2s, and 4-8-4s hauling longer, heavier trains on faster schedules. Something had to give.

A few hours after midnight on August 18, 1938, one of the big Northerns was easing down the 0.8 percent grade past Arkalon, Kansas, with eastbound freight No. 91. At the bottom of the grade, 12 hours of rain had swept away 20 panels of the deck timber bridge over the Cimarron River. The flood-prone Cimarron had long been an agony to Rock Island. The winding grade up out of the valley meant helpers on heavy trains both ways. The bridge itself was subject to frequent washouts, but this morning's was the last. The engine and a dozen cars plunged into the muddy water. The engineer was swept free, but the fireman was trapped in the cab until a hobo who happened to be riding the train dragged him to safety.

The line remained closed for a month until a temporary track could be laid over the muddy river bottoms and the engine and cars hauled away.

The disaster proved timely. The resulting realignment and the construction of a spectacular 1,269-foot steel bridge over the river—the famous "Samson of the Cimarron"—not only eliminated helpers, but cut almost 4 miles off the line and increased train speeds. It inaugurated a sweeping campaign of rebuilding and realignment under John Farrington that remade Rock Island.

Curves and grades, of which the road had more than its share, add to running time and fuel costs. A train squealing through a 4-degree curve (1,432-foot radius) at 10 miles per hour requires 70 percent more horsepower than the same train on straight track. It takes five times the force to lug a train up a 1 percent grade as it does to move it on level track. The $1.4 million Arkalon bypass, as it was called, saved about $100,000 a year, a return of 7 percent on investment. In this way, the savings realized from each project paid for the next.

Most of the rebuilding and realignment came to the Davenport–Kansas City line. John Barriger, in his 1930 inspection of the road, had recommended that much of the Iowa trackage be scrapped in favor of an entirely new 160-mile line cutting diagonally across the state. The price tag in Depression dollars: $18 million. The trustees caught their collective breath and instead approved a shopping list of shorter but significant relocations.

Seven projects between Davenport and Allerton, Iowa, alone carved 11 miles and 2,714 degrees of curvature from the original alignment. From Mercer to Mill Grove, Missouri, 15.1 new miles eliminated 411 degrees of curvature and bypassed a 1.58 percent grade.

Crews finished the Eldon, Missouri–Perlee, Iowa, relocation, moved on to Centerville–Paris, Iowa, then Paris–Floris, then Ainsworth–Brighton. In the end, almost 20 miles were carved from the Chicago–Kansas City line. The ruling grade in most districts was but 0.5 percent. Helpers were eliminated in most locations, and engine tonnage and train speeds increased. New overpasses and bridges replaced grade crossings and rickety trestles.

Most of the work was done by the end of World War II, though an important bypass north of Denver and a new line between Atlantic and Council Bluffs, Iowa, kept crews busy into the 1950s.

In November 1948, when documentary photographer Charles E. Rotkin took this aerial view, bustling El Reno, Oklahoma, was headquarters of the Rock Island's Southern Division. The 23-stall El Reno roundhouse was still dispatching steam to the four corners of the system along the Memphis–Tucumcari and Minneapolis–Fort Worth lines. The 100-foot turntable turned dozens of engines a day, and some 1,800 townspeople worked for the railroad. Today only weeds remain. *Standard Oil (New Jersey), Photographic Archives, University of Louisville*

Denver's 14th Street Viaduct offers a view of 4-8-2 No. 4030 as it heads from Rio Grande's Burnham roundhouse to Union Station on September 11, 1949, to pick up the passenger equipment for Train 26. Under an 1891 agreement, Rio Grande serviced and turned Rock Island power in the Mile High City. Paired tracks at right, beyond the communication line, were the joint Colorado & Southern–Santa Fe Railway passenger main. *George A. Trout photo, courtesy Denver Public Library, Western History Collection*

continued from page 95

The fight over ICC's reorganization plan went before the court for a final hearing in June 1944. Under the plan, the road's managers would select the board of directors. This did not fit Colnon's ambitions. The court waited a year and then approved reorganization. Immediately, the road's creditors filed an appeal. Acting like he already ran the raIlroad, Colnon began nosing around the purchasing department, diverting contracts that had once gone to the lowest bidder into the hands of his friends.

Congress entered the picture. Under the proposed Wheeler Bill, all action on railroad bankruptcies would halt—New Haven, Missouri Pacific, Rio Grande, Frisco, and Seaboard were still in bankruptcy, along with Rock Island—and the roads would be returned to their stockholders. The bill made its way through Congress and landed on the desk of President Harry S. Truman, who vetoed it.

Faced with the order to approve ICC's plan, the lower court dragged its feet. Colnon took the opportunity to propose his own plan, which was very generous to bondholders. Behind the scenes was Robert R. Young's Allegheny Corporation, a growing power in railroad finance, which was buying up Rock Island bonds. Once again, the circuit court ordered implementation of the ICC plan. Colnon had overstepped himself, the higher court warned.

On January 1, 1948, after 15 years, 6 months, and 23 days, the Rock Island finally emerged from bankruptcy as the Chicago, Rock Island & Pacific Rail*road*. In a decisive defeat for Colnon, the new board was composed almost entirely of representatives of major on-line industries. The eastern bankers were frozen out. John Farrington immediately became president, and the road embarked on a debt-reduction program, cutting first and

Loafing along just west of Manila, Colorado, at all of 15 miles per hour, BL2 No. 426 works the 14 cars of Train 26, the daily mixed out of Denver. On June 21, 1951, the branch-line unit has recently been retrofitted with a steam generator, qualifying it for local passenger runs. *Otto C. Perry photo, courtesy Denver Public Library, Western History Collection*

Some consider Rock Island's 5100s among the handsomest of all 4-8-4s. From an aesthetic viewpoint, there's little to criticize as No. 5114 rides the turntable at Silvis in 1952. Performance-wise, however, they were slippery and steamed hard, and veteran engine crews preferred the earlier 5000s. The last of the 4-8-4s went to the torch in 1955. *Charles Kerrigan photo, Tom Klinger collection*

Oil-burning No. 5100 storms through a Kansas town, giving a passable imitation of a passenger engine. Built for dual service but remembered mostly as freight haulers, the 5100s served out their last days in November 1952 on Trains 43 and 44, head-end runs west from Kansas City. *Author collection*

general mortgage bonds by almost half. A new hump yard was built at Silvis, Illinois. More diesels filled the ready tracks, and steamers joined the long storage lines.

Out on the high plains of western Kansas and eastern Colorado, where sudden storms could sweep away miles of telegraph wires, the road erected microwave towers, the first in railroading. Streamlined commuter coaches entered service. In 1949, earnings dropped severely, and across the nation railroad switchmen began clamoring for a 40-hour work week and an 18-cent hourly wage increase. Arbitration dragged on, then failed, and for the second time in six years President Truman ordered the army to run the railroads. The unions quickly settled, but it took months for traffic to recover.

Crops failed across the Southwest. Then, as so often happens, a period of too little rain was followed by a burst of too much. In spring 1951, heavy rains swept away bridges in Oklahoma and Kansas. Week after week, they continued, moving steadily eastward. Then on July 12, the Kansas River demolished Rock Island's Topeka Bridge. The *Rocket* was turned back to Kansas City, rising water pursuing it all the way. By evening, Rock Island's

Rock Island Marks Centennial With Continuing Program of Dieselization

A continuing program of dieselization keynotes the long-range planning of the Rock Island as it enters its second century of railroading this month.
Aided by a fleet of 95 ALCO-GE locomotives, this "railroad of planned progress" already has dieselized 85% of its operations. First to dieselize completely its suburban service into Chicago, the Rock Island selected ALCO-GE road switchers almost exclusively to handle this high-speed passenger service.
Whether in passenger or switching service, or heading up the crack ROCKET freights, economical ALCO-GE locomotives are helping the Rock Island to win more and more tonnage to the rails.

AMERICAN LOCOMOTIVE
and
GENERAL ELECTRIC

In 1952, the centennial of Rock Island's first train, *Modern Railroads* magazine devoted its October issue to a celebration of "A Century of Service." Major suppliers kicked in with congratulatory ads, including this two-page spread depicting the road's new FA freighters. The painting is by redoubtable railroad artist Howard Fogg. *Author collection*

Armourdale Yard, near the confluence of the Kansas and Missouri rivers, was under water. Hostlers parked the road's valuable diesels on the hump. Empty boxcars floated away and loaded cars disappeared to their roof lines. Within a day, Farrington and Downing B. Jenks, who had just become Rock Island's chief operating officer, were on the scene to direct recovery operations. For Jenks, it was baptism by mud. Kansas City's railroads needed days to dig out. The cost to Rock Island, including traffic lost, was almost $15 million. It was the worst disaster in the road's 99-year history. The flood was followed by massive crop failures throughout the Wheat Belt.

Nothing could dampen the spirit of the railroad's weeklong 100th anniversary celebration, held October 5–12, 1952. A train of dignitaries descended upon Rock Island for dedication of a new station. Within two months, the road would be, to all intents and purposes, dieselized.

Farrington was now nearing the end of his extraordinary career. In two decades, he had literally remade the Rock. The railroad had fought a war, emerged from bankruptcy, and spent more than $235 million to rebuild and reequip itself. Thousands of miles of track had been relaid with heavier rail. More than 3,500 miles were either signaled or under CTC. Steam was gone. *Rockets* ruled the rails. More than 3,300 new industrial plants had sprung up along the line.

At the end of 1955, Farrington retired, and Jenks assumed the presidency. Farrington was not quite finished with the Rock. He would remain on as chairman of the board. But other hands were on the throttle. And there were twists and turns in the road ahead.

Barely a week out of GE's Erie, Pennsylvania, plant in mid-October 1965, U25B No. 230 crosses the long approach to the Harry Truman Bridge from Birmingham, Missouri. Until Rock Island and Milwaukee Road built the $3 million bridge in 1944, Rock's trains arrived in Kansas City via a circuitous route that added 30 minutes to their schedules. *Bill Marvel*

SW900 No. 901, parked at Des Moines, Iowa, in September 1967, has somehow escaped the paint shop for 30 years and still wears its original steam-engine black. The offspring of a 1959 remanufacturing program that turned 1937-built 600-horsepower SWs into 900-horsepower SW900s, No. 901 will be rebuilt and renumbered yet again in 1971 to 1,200-horsepower No. 780. *Bill Marvel*

Fresh from EMD at LaGrange, Illinois, GP40 No. 4704 and two sisters are at Commerce City, inbound on the Belt Line for Rio Grande's North Yard. Rock Island built the 5-mile cutoff from Sandown Junction in 1951 to avoid a long trip through Denver's congested freight yards. *Ron Hill*

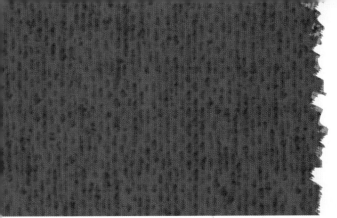

Freshly painted in the striking yellow-stripe scheme, No. 662, an ex–Union Pacific E9A, slows for the stop at 115th Street in Morgan Park. By October 1970, Rock Island's double-track suburban line is showing signs of neglect. *Paul Dolkos*

CHAPTER FIVE

THE ROAD TO RIDE

The Rock Island was usually not the shortest, nor the fastest, nor the most prosperous railroad between the cities it served. So it had to try harder.

Even in the worst of times, the railroad did its best to field a fleet that gave passengers a run for their money. And when times were flush, the Rock Island often ran ahead of the pack. It was among the first with onboard dining and streamliners. It innovated restlessly, if not always wisely. Its trains might run in the red, especially toward the end, but they ran.

As soon as the track was down and open for business in 1852, two daily trains left Chicago for Joliet. Within months the dozen passenger cars provided by contractors Henry Farnam and Joseph Sheffield could no longer meet demand, and 16 additional cars were ordered. Trains ran full, hauling passengers from Chicago's passenger house to the end of track, wherever that might be. By 1856 the road was advertised "the Shortest, Quickest and Safest Route" to Kansas and Nebraska—though it had reached neither destination. The roadbed was raw, the

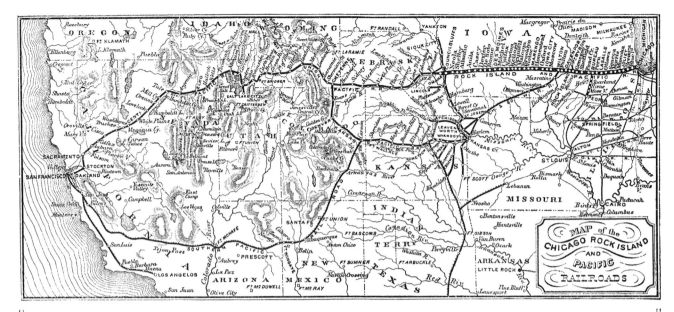

GREAT OVERLAND ROUTE
VIA
Chicago, Rock Island & Pacific Rail Road
FROM OCEAN TO OCEAN!
GREAT CENTRAL SHORT LINE BETWEEN CHICAGO AND OMAHA,
PASSING THROUGH DES MOINES, THE CAPITAL OF IOWA.
PURCHASE THROUGH TICKETS via ROCK ISLAND ROUTE.
A. M. SMITH, General Passenger Agent.   HUGH RIDDLE, General Superintendent.

Above: Rock Island's own territorial ambitions lay in the future in June 1870, when the road promoted itself in the pages of the *Travelers' Official Guide of the Railways and Steam Navigation Lines in the United States & Canada* as the "Central Short Line" between Chicago and the "Great Overland Route." Lines to Atchison and Kansas City, as yet unbuilt, appeared on its map but not in its timetables. *Author collection*

Opposite: In summer 1870, Rock Island offered two overnight trains a day each way between Chicago and its Union Pacific connection at Council Bluffs, plus Chicago–Peru and Des Moines–Council Bluffs accommodations. Hungry passengers could look forward to meal stops at Bureau, Davenport, and Avoca. *Author collection*

crude wooden benches were hard, but tens of thousands of immigrants were already riding Rock Island trains on the first leg of their journeys to the Great American Frontier. Within the decade, they would ship their produce to eastern markets via Rock Island.

Accommodations softened. By the mid-1880s, "The Great Rock Island Route"

promised patrons "the finest reclining chair cars in the world" and "that sense of personal security offered by a solid, thoroughly ballasted roadbed." Two daily trains ran all the way to Council Bluffs. Others fanned out to Minneapolis (via Minneapolis & St. Louis), Kansas City, and other points on the growing system.

A pioneer in onboard meal service west of Chicago, the road placed its first dining car in operation in May 1877. With the 1888 completion of its Colorado line, the road announced meal service on its all-vestibule Denver train, igniting a brief but vigorous "dining car war" with Union Pacific and Burlington. Those roads enjoyed the faster and more direct routes. If Rock Island could not outrun its competitors, it could match them luxury for luxury. In 1898 the road inaugurated Trains 41 and 42, the

217 CHICAGO, ROCK ISLAND AND PACIFIC RAILROAD.

GENERAL OFFICERS.

JOHN F. TRACY, President, Chicago, Ill.
HUGH RIDDLE, Gen. Superintendent, Chicago, Ill.
P. A. HALL, Assistant General Supt., Chicago, Ill.
W. G. PURDY, Cashier, Chicago, Ill.
F. A. SHERMAN, Auditor, Chicago, Ill.

A. M. SMITH, General Passenger Agent, Chicago, Ill.
E. ST. JOHN, Gen. Ticket Agent, Chicago, Ill.
L. VIELE, General Freight Agent, Chicago, Ill.
E. H. JOHNSON, Chief Engineer, Chicago, Ill.

A. KIMBALL, Asst. Supt. Iowa Division, (East,) Davenport, Ia.
H. F. ROYCE, Asst. Supt. Iowa Division (West,) Council Bluffs, Ia.
ALLEN MAUVEL, Purchasing Agent, Chicago, Ill.
JOHN T. SANDFORD, New York Agent, 257 Broadway, N.Y

Time Schedule in effect May 8, 1870.

Trains going West.

Illinois Division.

Illinois Division.	Mls	Pacific Express except Sunday	Peru Accom'n except Sunday.	Pacific Express except Saturday
Lve. Chicago[1]		10 00 A.M.	5 00 P.M.	10 00 P.M.
Englewood[2]	7	10 25 "	5 25 "	10 25 "
Blue Island	16	10 51 "	5 50 "	10 48 "
Bremen	24	11 12 "	6 11 "	......
Mokena	30	11 27 "	6 28 "	......
Joliet[3]	40	11 57 A.M	6 52 "	11 45 P.M.
Minooka	51	12 26 P.M.	7 25 "	12 10 A.M.
Morris	61	12 55 "	7 54 "	12 36 "
Seneca	71	1 20 "	8 20 "	......
Marseilles	76	1 31 "	8 33 "	......
Ottawa	84	1 50 "	8 55 "	1 30 "
Utica	94	2 13 "	9 20 "	1 53 "
La Salle[4]	99	2 25 "	9 35 "	2 05 "
Peru	100		9 45 P.M.	2 15 "
Bureau[5]	114	‡3 15 "	ARRIVE.	3 00 "

Peoria Branch:

	Mls	Pacific Express		Pacific Express
Henry	128	4 15 "		3 43 "
Sparland	135	4 33 "		4 05 "
Chillicothe	143	4 55 "		4 30 "
Peoria[6]	161	5 45 arr.		5 30 arr.

	Mls	Pacific Express		Pacific Express
Tiskilwa[7]	122	4 00 "		3 21 A.M.
Pond Creek[7]	128	4 13 "		......
Sheffield	136	4 32 "		3 54 "
Annawan	146	4 51 "		......
Atkinson	152	5 02 "		......
Geneseo	159	5 20 "		4 45 "
Colona	170	5 45 "		5 15 "
Moline	179	6 12 "		5 37 "
Rock Island[8]	182	6 20 P.M.		5 50 "

Iowa Div.—East.

	Mls	Pacific Express		Pacific Express
Lve. Davenport	183	*7 00 P.M.		‡6 30 A.M.
Walcott	195	7 36 "		7 10 "
Fulton	199			7 22 "
Wilton[9]	208	8 10 "		7 46 "

Oskaloosa Div. B'ch:

	Mls	Pacific Express		Pacific Express
Muscatine	220	8 55 P.M.		8 40 "
Ononwa	233			9 20 "
Fredonia	239			9 40 "
Ainsworth	250			10 15 "
Wash'gton	257			10 35 "

	Mls	Pacific Express		Pacific Express
Moscow	211	8 22 "		7 55 A.M.
Atalissa	216			8 10 "
West Liberty	221	8 47 "		8 24 "
Downey	227			8 40 "
Iowa City	237	9 25 "		9 06 "
Oxford	252			9 47 "
Homestead	257			10 02 "
Marengo	267	10 40 "		10 30 "
Victor	279			11 04 "
Brooklyn	287	11 32 P.M.		11 45 A.M.
Malcom	293			12 00 NO'N
Grinnell	302	12 10 A.M.		12 25 P.M.
Kellogg	313			1 00 "
Newton	322			1 23 "
Colfax	334	1 30 "		1 55 "
Mitchelville	340			2 12 "

Iowa Div.—West.

	Mls	Pacific Express	Accom'n	Pacific Express
Lve. Des Moines[10]	357	2 30 "	7 00 A.M.	3 00 "
Boone	372		7 58 "	3 44 "
De Soto	379	3 28 "	8 30 "	4 03 "
Dexter	392		9 17 "	4 23 "
Casey	408	4 43 "	10 25 "	5 25 "
Adair	415		10 55 "	5 45 "
Anita	422		11 25 "	6 04 "
Atlantic	436	6 00 "	12 20 P.M.	6 43 "
Avoca	455	‡7 00 "	†1 50 "	*7 50 "
Shelby	463	7 24 "	2 25 "	8 12 "
Neola	474		3 20 "	8 40 "
Council Bluffs[11]	490	8 50 "	4 55 P.M.	9 40 "
Missouri River	493	9 00 A.M. ARRIVE.	ARRIVE.	9 50 P.M. ARRIVE.

Trains going East.

Iowa Div.—West.

Iowa Div.—West.	Fares	Pacific Express except Sunday	Accom'n except Sunday.	Pacific Express except Saturday
Lve. Missouri River		5 50 A.M.		4 50 P.M.
Council Bluffs[11]		6 00 "	12 15 P.M.	5 00 "
Neola		6 50 "	1 35 "	......
Shelby		7 24 "	2 25 "	......
Avoca		‡8 10 "	3 15 "	*7 00 "
Atlantic		9 03 "	4 25 "	7 50 "
Anita		9 40 "	5 15 "	......
Adair		10 02 "	5 45 "	......
Casey		10 25 "	6 15 "	9 12 "
Dexter		11 10 "	7 25 "	......
De Soto		11 45 "	8 16 "	10 32 "
Boone		12 04 P.M.	8 45 "	......
Des Moines[10]		12 50 "	9 45 P.M.	11 35 P.M.

Iowa Div.—East.

	Fares	Pacific Express	Accom'n	Pacific Express
Lve. Mitchellville		1 40 "		......
Colfax		1 55 "		......
Newton		2 30 "		1 02 A.M
Kellogg		2 58 "		......
Grinnell		3 32 "		......
Malcom		4 00 "		......
Brooklyn		‡4 35 "		2 35 "
Victor		4 48 "		......
Marengo		5 22 "		3 30 "
Homestead		5 50 "		......
Oxford		6 03 "		......
Iowa City		6 42 "		4 50 "
Downey		7 08 "		......
West Liberty		7 24 "		5 25 "
Atalissa		7 37 "		......
Moscow		7 50 "		......

Oskaloosa Div. B'ch:

	Fares	Pacific Express		Pacific Express
Wash'ton		5 30 P.M.		......
Ainsworth		5 52 "		......
Fredonia		6 20 "		......
Ononwa		6 40 "		......
Muscatine		7 20 "		5 10 lve

	Fares	Pacific Express		Pacific Express
Wilton[9]		8 10 "		5 58 "
Fulton		8 33 "		......
Walcott		8 45 "		6 27 "
Davenport		*9 45 "		‡7 20 "

Illinois Division.

	Fares	Pacific Express		Pacific Express
Lve. Rock Island[8]		10 00 "		7 30 "
Moline		10 08 "		7 38 "
Colona		10 31 "		8 07 "
Geneseo		10 58 "		8 38 "
Atkinson				8 54 "
Annawan				9 07 "
Sheffield		11 52 P.M.		9 28 "
Pond Creek[7]				9 50 "
Tiskilwa[7]		12 25 A.M.		10 05 "

Peoria Branch:

	Fares	Pacific Express		Pacific Express
Peoria[6]		10 30 P.M.		8 10 A.M.
Chillicothe		11 20 "		9 03 "
Sparland		11 43 P.M.		9 26 "
Henry		12 02 A.M		9 46 "

	Fares	Pacific Express	Accom'n	Pacific Express
Bureau[5]		1 00 "	LEAVE.	10 40 "
Peru		1 30 "	5 00 A.M.	11 15 "
La Salle[4]		1 40 "	5 10 "	11 25 "
Utica		1 53 "	5 24 "	11 38 A.M.
Ottawa		2 16 "	5 44 "	12 00 NO'N
Marseilles		......	6 12 "	12 18 P.M.
Seneca		2 48 "	6 26 "	12 30 "
Morris		3 13 "	6 55 "	12 55 "
Minooka		3 40 "	7 20 "	1 20 "
Joliet[3]		4 07 "		1 46 "
Mokena		......	8 23 "	2 13 "
Bremen		......	8 43 "	2 22 "
Blue Island		5 10 "	9 04 "	2 47 "
Englewood[2]		5 35 "	9 25 "	3 10 "
Chicago[1]		6 00 A.M. ARRIVE.	9 50 A.M ARRIVE.	3 35 P.M. ARRIVE.

CONNECTIONS.

[1] With Railways diverging from Chicago, and Steamers on Lake Michigan.

[2] At Englewood with Lake Shore and Mich. Southern, and Pittsburg, Fort Wayne and Chicago Railways.

[3] At Joliet with Chicago and Alton Railroad, and Joliet Branch Michigan Central Railway.

[4] At La Salle with Illinois Central Railroad and steamers to St. Louis.

[5] At Bureau with Branch to Peoria.

[6] At Peoria with Peoria, Pekin and Jacksonville Railroad; Steamers on the Illinois Riv.; and Toledo, Peoria and Warsaw Railway.

[7] At Pond Creek with Chicago, Burlington and Quincy Railroad.

[8] At Rock Island with Western Union RR, and Bridge over the Mississippi River, connecting Illinois with Iowa Division, also with Steamers on the Mississippi River.

[9] At Wilton with Branch for Muscatine, Washington, &c.

[10] At Des Moines with Des Moines Valley Railroad.

[11] At Council Bluffs and Omaha with Missouri River Steamers for Benton and all upper Missouri River trading posts, also with Union Pacific Railroad for Cheyenne, Denver, Central City, Santa Fe, New Mexico, Ogden, Salt Lake and all mining districts, and all points in Upper and Lower California, and with ocean steamers for all points on the Pacific coast.

—o—

STANDARD OF TIME.

The Clock in the Superintendent's Office at CHICAGO will be taken as the standard time of the Road.

—o—

* Supper. † Dinner. ‡ Breakfast.

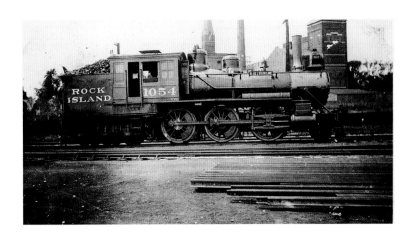

Like several Chicago railroads in the 1890s, Rock Island acquired a small fleet of "Forney" suburban tank engines to handle growing commuter business. With the arrival of steel coaches, the six "teakettles," as riders called them—not always affectionately—were replaced by Atlantics, Ten-Wheelers, and finally Pacifics. *Author collection*

Rocky Mountain Limited, offering 28-hour 30-minute service to Denver/Colorado Springs. Pullman-built equipment included chair cars, Palace sleeping cars, buffet-library cars, and a 64-foot diner. The price of a meal was 75 cents. By 1902, the schedule had been cut to 24 hours.

With completion of the Santa Rosa line and connection with the El Paso & Northeastern the same year, the road introduced the *Golden State Limited*, offering first-class service to California. By 1912 passengers were treated to daily Victrola recitals in the parlor car, while daily news updates were available by wire. Later known simply as the *Golden State*, it remained Rock Island's flagship almost to the end.

By 1916 travelers out of Chicago could choose from 10 daily east-west trains, all of

© Colorado Historical Society

Somewhere on the plains of eastern Colorado around 1898, the *Rocky Mountain Limited* has paused behind long-legged 4-4-0 No. 1112 while William Henry Jackson focuses the image on the ground glass of his 8x10 view camera. The picture will make fine publicity for the new Pullman-built train, which offers sleepers, chair cars, a buffet-library, and 75-cent meals in the diner. *Courtesy Colorado Historical Society, Jackson Collection scan #20103775*

Lucky was the Chicago visitor in 1897 who had a copy of the Poole Brothers' bird's-eye map of the Loop area. It showed all hotels, principal office buildings, theaters, cable and electric street railways, and railroad stations, including Rock Island's, where "all elevated trains" stop. The inset view, lower left, shows the station. *Library of Congress Geography and Map Division*

them competitive. The road dominated the Minneapolis–Kansas City corridor and had the Chicago–Peoria business to itself. Periodically, the road upgraded its service, re-equipping its top limiteds, whose cars were then passed down to lesser trains. In 1929, during one of these house cleanings, the *Golden State*, *Iowa-Nebraska Limited*, and *Rocky Mountain Limited* all received new sun-parlor cars with generous picture windows and Pullman sleepers with upper-berth windows, the first on any railroad. The *Rocky Mountain Limited* offered male travelers barber and valet service.

Rock Island passenger service through the mid-1930s underwent a slow but steady evolution. Then came the revolution. The road had dabbled in internal combustion for a decade, mostly on branch lines where a locomotive and a coach or two was an unnecessary expense. Gas-electric "doodlebugs" and a couple of homebuilt experiments cut costs dramatically, particularly where they could drag a few freight cars along the branch.

In 1934 Chicago, Burlington & Quincy's *Zephyr* hit the rails, and railroading changed forever. Within two years, streamliners were polishing the rails of Union Pacific, Boston & Maine, Illinois Central, New Haven, and Milwaukee. A year later, Southern Pacific's gorgeous *Daylights* and Santa Fe's famous *Chiefs* made their debut. Even Alton, Reading, and Baltimore & Ohio were in the game.

Rock Island responded to the *Zephyr* by tarting up one of its 4-8-4s. Shop forces at Silvis painted the boiler jacket of No. 5040 bright red, the smokebox aluminum, and white-striped the wheels. The locomotive took over the *Golden State Limited*, Rock Island to Kansas City.

This was a stopgap. In 1937 John Farrington announced that the road would enter the streamliner sweepstakes with a fleet of six diesel-powered, all-stainless-steel trains, each to be named *Rocket* in honor of the locomotive that had hauled that first passenger train 38 miles from Chicago to Joliet in October 1852.

Farrington had his eye on more than the competition. Employee morale was sagging. Trains were chronically late. Annual passenger revenues had fallen to less than a fifth of the $30 million the road was earning during the 1920s. Bankruptcy dragged on. "The hardest thing we had to do was to live down Rock

Island's reputation," he said.

The new *Rockets* would go a long way toward doing that.

Rocket Years

The story of Rock Island's passenger trains after 1936 is the story of the *Rockets*.

Though the Rock was a little late getting into streamliners, once it got in there was nothing hesitant about its approach. Paid for with cash generated from those Farrington scrap drives and by equipment trusts, the new trains were state of the art. Up front, the six 1,200-horsepower Electro-Motive TAs were a brand-new model, unique to Rock Island. The road asked Electro-Motive to create a design as eye-catching as Santa Fe's famous warbonnet scheme, and stylists responded

with a sleek and rakish slant-nose diesel-electric with two-tone maroon and red nose and gleaming stainless-steel flanks. The TAs looked as speedy standing in the station as they did out on the line. And they *were* speedy, geared for a sizzling 115 miles an hour.

Delivered in two 4-car sets and four 3-car sets, the 20 original cars were of stainless-steel shot-welded construction, eliminating rows of unsightly rivets. Riding lower than standard heavyweights, they had fluted sides

In September 1930, T-27 No. 1305 is one of a handful of superheated Ten-Wheelers still hauling commuters out of the big La Salle Street train shed. Brooks-built in 1902, the engine wears destination boards and has a cut-down tender for visibility. *Otto C. Perry photo, courtesy Denver Public Library, Western History Collection*

Barely a month and a half old in September 1930, the first of Rock Island's eventual 1,033 diesel locomotives switches at the La Salle Street station. Copied from identical New York Central engines, No. 10000 used an Ingersoll-Rand diesel to charge a 126-ton set of batteries that in turn drove traction motors. The pioneer lasted until 1952. *Otto C. Perry photo, courtesy Denver Public Library, Western History Collection*

for added strength and articulated trucks—one set of wheels supporting two cars—to reduce weight. Interiors were bright and elegant, with blue-gray ceilings, blue walls, and blue and gold carpets, or peach ceilings, beige walls, and blue carpets. Four-car sets had kitchenettes with attached 32-seat dinettes; three-car sets had 28-seat dinettes.

When the first three-unit set arrived in mid-summer, 1937, it was dispatched on a speed run to Denver, clicking off the 1,073 miles at an average 67 miles per hour. Then it went on a publicity tour of the system, during which tens of thousands trooped through the cars or gawked and waved from trackside.

The first of the new trains, the three-car *Texas Rocket*, entered service August 29, 1937, on Burlington–Rock Island's joint Dallas–Houston operation, where it ran opposite Fort Worth & Denver's *Sam Houston Zephyr*. Three weeks later, the first four-car trainset began twice daily Chicago–Peoria service. It was followed within the week by a daily four-car Chicago–Des Moines *Rocket*. Four days later, a pair of three-car *Rocket* sets entered Minneapolis–Kansas City service. The final three-car set began Kansas City–Denver operation in mid-October.

Originally, two trainsets were to cover the Denver operation, but one almost immediately was reassigned to the Burlington–Rock Island. That left but a single trainset for the long Denver run, over track that was not the best, and departures were cut back to three times a week. With Santa Fe and Union Pacific both offering daily service, response to the Denver *Rocket* was less than enthusiastic. The train was transferred to Kansas City–Oklahoma City service, and Rock Island began making plans for another Colorado train, this one to run all the way from Chicago on improved roadbed. It would be called the *Rocky Mountain Rocket*.

With the exception of the Denver train's false start, Farrington's gamble was paying off. In their first year of operation, the *Rockets* earned almost half a million dollars, returning 55 percent on investment. In three years they had paid for themselves.

Greg Stout's comprehensive *Route of the Rockets: Rock Island in the Streamlined Era* offers a route-by-route and almost year-by-year account of the rise and eventual fall of the *Rockets*. As patronage grew, the articulated sets proved small and inflexible and were replaced by single-unit cars. Trains grew longer. TAs gave way to larger, more powerful

Passengers in the observation-parlor car *Pikes Peak* still have the Rocky Mountains in view as EMC TA No. 606 flies eastward with the Budd-built Denver–Kansas City *Rocket*. Less than a month old on November 18, 1937, the three-car streamliner will soon be shifted to Kansas City–Oklahoma City service. In late 1939, its place will be taken by the new Chicago–Denver *Rocky Mountain Rocket*. *Otto C. Perry photo, courtesy Denver Public Library, Western History Collection*

Train 509, the short-lived Kansas City–Denver *Rocket*, makes its Topeka stop behind TA No. 606 in early 1938. The three-car Budd-built train ran tri-weekly, not often enough to attract steady patronage. By February the Budd-built equipment was shifted to a shorter Kansas City–Oklahoma City run. Denver had to wait another year to get its own *Rocky Mountain Rocket* and then the equipment ran daily to Chicago. *Tom Lee photo, Tom Klinger collection*

Performing work for which it was designed, A-B6 No. 750 leads the Colorado Springs section of Train 8, the *Rocky Mountain Rocket*, away from 14,115-foot Pikes Peak and toward a rendezvous with its Denver counterpart at Limon. On January 10, 1943, it's a good bet that all three cars are filled with servicemen from nearby Camp Carson. *Otto C. Perry photo, courtesy Denver Public Library, Western History Collection*

Electro-Motive E3s and E6s, and Alco DLs. Numbers and routes were shuffled and re-shuffled. New *Rockets* set out for new terminals as Memphis, Little Rock, and Amarillo became streamliner destinations.

With inauguration of the Memphis–Amarillo *Choctaw Rocket* in November 1940, Rock Island for once beat the competition. Parallel Missouri Pacific would not send streamliners over even part of the route for eight years. Although the *Choctaw Rocket* was a modern train from coupler to coupler, in one respect it was a throwback. The lead coach on the train was partitioned to provide an eight-seat Jim Crow section for the accommodation of African Americans over the route. So it would remain—as would Jim Crow coaches on *Rocket* trains serving Texas and Oklahoma—until 1954 when the Supreme Court declared separate but equal facilities in interstate commerce unconstitutional.

Only the wandering-but-scenic Kansas City–St. Louis line, which had made do with daily gas-electrics since the mid-1930s, missed out on *Rocket* service. Instead, Rock joined with Burlington to offer a twice-daily *Zephyr-Rocket* from Minneapolis-St. Paul. It was the last new streamliner introduced by Rock Island until after the war.

At the end of 1942, Rock Island's passenger fleet numbered 52 streamlined cars. Wartime demand for steel meant no new passenger equipment would be available for the duration, but in 1945 the road cobbled

The Limon Do-Si-Do

Busy moments at Limon, Colorado, where, on July 7, 1940, the Colorado Springs section of Train 8, the *Rock Mountain Rocket*, has just pulled in behind A-B 750. Just visible in the background is E6A No. 629 with the section from Denver. Within 15 minutes, the engines will shuffle cars and the combined train will be on its way to Chicago. *Otto C. Perry photo, courtesy Denver Public Library, Western History Collection*

When it spiked down rails west out of Goodland, Kansas, Rock Island predecessor Chicago, Kansas & Nebraska had two destinations in view: Colorado Springs, where the Colorado Midland Railway was building a standard gauge line into the Rockies, and larger, more prosperous Denver, the state capital, with firm ties to the Union Pacific system. However, the two cities were 69 miles apart and not on a direct line. If the Rock was to serve both, it would have to build—or acquire—separate lines.

The fork in the road came out on the high plains, at Lake Siding, where Rock Island's Colorado Springs line crossed Union Pacific's Kansas City–Denver line. For several months after arriving at Colorado Springs, the Rock's Denver-bound trains turned north there and crawled over Palmer Divide on Rio Grande rails. But in 1889, the road negotiated trackage rights into mile-high Denver over UP from Lake Siding, now renamed Limon. Rock's passenger trains could now serve both cities in relative ease.

Relative ease usually meant splitting westbound trains in Limon, where the Rock had a small roundhouse, and sending each section on to its own destination. Eastbounds were recombined in Limon. With the diesel-powered *Rocky Mountain Rocket*, the railroad worked out an interesting variation of this maneuver.

Key to the process was a pair of unique locomotives, essentially 1,000-horsepower B units equipped with cabs and baggage compartments in place of second prime movers. Numbered 750 and 751, these Electro-Motive A-Bs ran multiple-unit behind standard A units. When the westbound *Rocket* arrived in Limon, the A unit uncoupled,

pulled forward, and the train was reshuffled into Denver and Colorado Springs sections. The E-unit then left for Denver via UP, and the A-B set out on the Rock Island for Colorado Springs.

Eastbound, it was more complicated. The section from the Springs usually pulled in first, stopping short of the UP junction. The A-B unit and Railway Post Office (RPO) car uncoupled. When the Denver train arrived, the E-unit uncoupled, leaving its train short of the crossing, and pulled forward. The A-B and Springs RPO then coupled behind the E-unit, and the two units and RPO car backed down and coupled onto the Denver RPO, coaches, and diner. The combination pulled forward and backed down onto the waiting Colorado Springs section. In a final move, the E-unit, A-B unit, RPOs, coaches, diner, and Colorado Springs train pulled forward, then backed down and coupled onto the remaining Denver sleepers on the UP line.

With the entire train now assembled, the engineer tested his air and whistled off for Goodland and points east. Some 15 minutes were scheduled for this complicated series of moves.

In 1948 the baggage compartments were eliminated from the A-Bs and a second diesel prime mover installed, making them the equivalent of standard E-units. By the mid-1960s, the *Rocky Mountain Rocket* was running its last miles. The A-Bs were assigned to other trains and eventually to commuter service. Doubtless, few commuters understood what these strange, flat-faced locomotives were doing on the head ends of their trains.

More interesting than the Alco RS-3 shuffling commuter cars at 12th Street in Chicago in May 1964 are the first three cars, an early Budd-built articulated set for *Rocket* service. Trailing are unique St. Louis Car–built commuter coaches, featuring low-level entry and double doors. *Marty Bernard*

together a new Minneapolis–Houston *Twin Star Rocket* from its existing fleet. Business was good and getting better. The 15 *Rockets* together ran 3,680,673 miles in 1947, earning more than $10 million, an average of $2.73 per train-mile. On every 1,075-mile dash to Colorado, the *Rocky Mountain Rocket* was pulling in more than $3,600. By 1948 new cars were rolling out of Pullman-Standard's plant by the dozens, and Rock Island, with partner Southern Pacific, re-equipped the extra-fare *Golden State* in handsome red and silver and put it on an accelerated 45-hour schedule. Originally, the cars were to make up a newer, even more luxurious train over the Chicago–Los Angeles route, a train with a strange history.

The *Golden Rocket*, as the new streamliner was to be named, was not a replacement for the daily *Golden State*. It would run only three times a week. In place of convenience, it would offer speed, covering the same 2,324-mile route in just under 40 hours, and a travel experience few trains could match. It would be in every way Rock Island's dream train.

Orders for the $1.5-million 11-car trains—one for each road—were placed with Pullman-Standard in late 1945 for early 1947 delivery. Stylists and designers immediately set to work. Exterior colors were SP red and Rock Island stainless steel. Interiors were to carry bright Southwest colors—terracotta, turquoise, bright reds, and deep blues. The *Fiesta* coach diner would feature curtains with Apache patterns, hand-carved tables and chairs, a red-tile floor, and a simulated-adobe bar adorned with Mexican pottery and colorful woven serapes. The more sedate first-class diner would be tastefully trimmed in copper. Mexican folk masks would stoically look on as patrons ordered from menu offerings as good as the best—and most expensive—restaurants.

Carl Byoir & Associates, one of the world's most prestigious advertising and public relations firms, quietly began cranking up the publicity machine for the train's mid-June 1947 launch. There would be a big splash in *Holiday* magazine, followed by a national press campaign. The train would begin its first run at the famous Hollywood and Vine intersection in the heart of glamorous Los

Angeles. Plenty of movie stars would be on board as the gleaming streamliner made its stately way along Pacific Electric street trackage to Los Angeles Union Station—the last of the great American train stations. Then the *Golden Rocket* would take to the main line for the run to Chicago.

Abruptly, Southern Pacific cancelled its set and dropped out of the project. Rock Island announced a postponement because of "equipment difficulties." In truth, without SP's participation, the *Golden Rocket* was dead on the track.

SP's problem was not the expense but the schedule. Rock Island's western partner made most of its *Golden State* revenue from sunbirds on their way to winter resorts in Arizona. Before the war intervened, in fact, the two roads had briefly fielded an all-Pullman wintertime Chicago–Phoenix train

on a convenient every-other-day schedule. By contrast, the *Golden Rocket*'s timetable would have stranded passengers in Phoenix in the wee hours.

And so the new cars were shuffled into the consist of the improved, faster, and more

continued on page 122

Overleaf: Frost lies on the ties, and folks are bundled against the Chicago cold as H15-44 No. 400 rolls past Beverly Hills station, otherwise known as 91st Street, on the last day of 1964. Fairbanks-Morse No. 400 and sister No. 401 are rarities in Rock Island suburban service at this late date: They were actually purchased to haul commuters. *Marty Bernard*

John Farrington's gamble has paid off. The original 1937 *Rocket* sets have paid back their investment 10 times over by 1948, and the train's builder, Philadelphia's Budd Company, congratulates itself and the railroad with a centerfold ad in the February 21, 1948, issue of the trade journal *Railway Age*. For bean-counting executives, the message is not in the gorgeous illustration by Iowa-born artist Leslie Ragan, but in the fine print: average expense per mile for the *Peoria Rocket*, $.897 cents; average operating profit per mile, $1.579. *Author collection*

Paid for themselves ten times in ten years

On September 19th, 1937, the Rock Island placed the all-stainless steel, Budd-built, Peoria Rocket in service.

One week later its all-stainless counterpart, the Des Moines Rocket, began operating between Chicago, the Tri-Cities and Des Moines.

For ten years, now, they have averaged a net operating profit per year exceeding their combined purchase price of $804,000.

Meeting an annual schedule assignment of 500,000 miles, you can be sure they don't spend much time in the shop. The ruggedness built into them with all-stainless steel construction and Budd design, keeps these trains where they belong — on the rails, earning a profit for their owners. Car availability: Peoria Rocket 98%, Des Moines Rocket 99%.

The Budd Company, Philadelphia.

Budd

PEORIA ROCKET

Lv. Peoria	7:00 AM	
Ar. Chicago	9:40 AM	
Lv. Chicago	10:35 AM	
Ar. Peoria	1:10 PM	
Lv. Peoria	3:00 PM	
Ar. Chicago	5:45 PM	
Lv. Chicago	7:00 PM	
Ar. Peoria	9:35 PM	

161 miles per trip—daily total 644 miles
Average speed 62 miles per hour
Daily service—10 hours, 35 minutes
*Average expense per mile . . $0.897
Average revenue per mile . . $2.476
Operating profit per mile . . . $1.579

DES MOINES ROCKET

Lv. Des Moines	7:00 AM	
Ar. Chicago	1:00 PM	
Lv. Chicago	5:00 PM	
Ar. Des Moines	11:00 PM	

358 miles per trip—daily total 716 miles
Average speed 60 miles per hour. Nine stops.
Daily service—12 hours
*Average expense per mile . . $0.927
Average revenue per mile . . $2.707
Operating profit per mile . . . $1.780

*Computed from the inauguration of each train thru Oct. 31, 1947

continued from page 119
luxurious *Golden State*. The last of the *Rockets* failed to leave the launch pad.

Experiments

Just as warbonnet *Chiefs* came to be associated with the Santa Fe and stainless-steel *Zephyrs* symbolized the Burlington, the maroon and silver *Rockets* became the public face of the Rock Island, for better or worse. As railroads began their long retreat from the passenger business, *Rocket* service declined, and with it public image of the railroad.

A failure in intercity service, all three of EMD's ultralightweight *Aerotrains* ended up in suburban service, inflicting their rough ride and narrow doors on long-suffering commuters. On April 21, 1965, LWT12 No. 2 pulls into Englewood Union Station, just a year away from its retirement to the National Railway Museum in Green Bay, Wisconsin. *Marty Bernard*

Business was still healthy in 1951. The law creating the interstate highway system was still five years in the future, and Rock Island's *Rockets* earned almost $8 million that year. The *Peoria Rocket* alone brought in $4.55 a mile, more than enough to cover its costs. But the trend was clear. In 1947, the *Rockets* had earned more than $10 million. Since 1949, the road had discontinued 5,247 passenger train miles; another 1,270 train-miles had been cut from suburban service.

Dining car operations were particularly worrisome. The road was spending more than a dollar on wages and food for every dollar its dining car stewards took in. By 1952 annual dining car losses topped $1 million.

In July 1951, John Farrington ordered

In one of those strange combinations of motive power that only Rock Island seemed to conjure up, FP-7A No. 407—followed by an F7B, an FB-1, and an RS-3—creep into Belleville, Kansas, with the 39 cars of freight No. 81 for Denver on August 21, 1956. *Tom Lee photo, Tom Klinger collection*

his executive assistant, Merle J. Reynolds, to find out what was wrong with dining car service and fix it. Reynolds rode some trains and nosed around on-line commissaries and quickly discovered that cars were being stocked with food that was never eaten; more than half spoiled or just vanished before the end of the run. He wondered, without onboard kitchens how did the airlines manage to feed passengers? Visits to the U. S. Air Force and to General Foods and other big institutional meal providers led him to the answer: precooked frozen meals. Instead of preparing individual meals to order en route, airlines prepared items in advance in a few central kitchens, froze them, then heated them on en route. Offer a limited menu, and cut costs and prices.

The Chicago commissary was re-equipped, and 18 smaller commissaries were established around the system. Warming ovens were installed in diners, and cooks and waiters were retrained. Paper napkins replaced cloth, placemats replaced tablecloths. China gave way to plastic plates, silverware to stainless steel. The railroad took its trademark off utensils to discourage souvenir hunters.

The new order began—fittingly, some thought—on April 1, 1952. Within a few weeks, passengers on most trains out of La Salle Street could order Swiss steak for $2 or something called a "poor man's steak" for $2.75. Only the *Golden State* kept full dining service.

The food was adequate and the prices were right. Diners actually spent more, and there were more of them. Pampered passengers on the *Peoria Rocket*, who always seemed to have management's ear, complained about the placemats, and linen returned to tables on that train. However, losses fell by 20 percent, to about $80,000 a month. Most of the changes became permanent, and worse was to come.

Restlessly cutting corners, the Rock in 1953 bought the first two of what would become a handful of Budd rail diesel cars (RDCs). The pair replaced the *Choctaw Rocket* on the 132-mile Little Rock–Oklahoma City run, saving the road the cost of a locomotive and full crew. Occasionally dragging a round-end observation car over the line, they were dubbed—perhaps inevitably—the *Choctaw Rockettes*. A conventional train continued to work the Little Rock–Memphis schedule, and an Electro-Motive GP7 or BL2 hauled a coach, a sleeper, and a string of head-end cars from Oklahoma City out to Amarillo. By

continued on page 126

The view from Roosevelt Road on June 2, 1971, takes in E8A No. 652 backing down to La Salle Street with a nameless Train 5, a 5:35 departure for Rock Island, and A-B6 No. 751 departing with bi-levels on suburban No. 301. *Paul C. Hunnell*

E3A No. 626 on May 30, 1958, descends on McFarland, Kansas, once a busy division point, with Train 509, the *Kansas City Rocket*—formerly the *Texas Rocket.* That third car, an RDC-3 coach, will continue solo south of Enid, Oklahoma, to Fort Worth. *Tom Lee photo, Tom Klinger collection*

continued from page 123

1955 the RDCs were running the full 762 miles from Memphis to Amarillo, the longest RDC run in the country. However, high plains blizzards often stopped them dead, and the road soon removed the engines, rebuilt them as conventional coaches, and folded them into regular consists.

A third RDC joined the fleet in 1954 and two more in 1956. All found similar employment. One was cut into the westbound *Imperial* out of Kansas City. At Enid, Oklahoma, it split off and went its own way, sometimes with a baggage-coach-observation car tied behind, as the *Kansas City Rocket* went to Fort Worth. By 1964 all five RDCs were stripped of their prime movers and ran as conventional Railway Post Office (RPO) coaches on regular passenger trains.

In an even more radical attempt to cut losses and rejuvenate Rock Island's passenger business, in 1954 Farrington announced the road would purchase a radical new train from ACF, formerly American Car & Foundry. Based upon the low-riding Spanish Talgos and costing $600,000, the new *Jet Rocket*, as it was to be oxymoronically named, would replace the *Peoria Rocket*, whisking some 300 passengers along in reclining reserved seats (at reserved-seat prices). Meals would be served airline-style right at the seats. Because the cars rode on guided axles and were suspended to tilt on curves, there would be nary a bump or splash. Farrington foresaw *Jet Rockets* also replacing the *Twin Star* and *Rocky Mountain Rockets*.

Plans were to haul the four-car train behind conventional diesels. But in 1955, General Motors announced its own ultra-lightweight *Aerotrain*, powered by a new diesel rated at 1,200 horsepower (the same as the original *Rocket* TAs). Styled by a design team led by GM's Harley Earl, the unit looked like a '57 Chevy. *Aerotrain*'s cars were wider versions of GM's standard 40-passenger intercity buses riding on four-wheel underframes. Rock Island acquired one of the LWT12s (indicating lightweight 1,200 horsepower) for its *Jet Rocket*.

The ACF-built *Jet Rocket* was dispatched on the usual promotional tour and on February 11, 1956, placed in Peoria service. Named the *Peorian*, the new train was immediately unpopular with patrons and employees alike. It was noisy and rough-riding. At station stops, passengers in the low-slung seats looked out and saw only shoes and ankles. On the other hand, the closed-circuit TV camera mounted in the cab caught some hair-raising scenes of near-misses at grade crossings. It was soon disconnected. The lightweight train failed to trip the railroad's signals, and high speeds and rapid deceleration soon burned out the disc brakes.

Patrons clamored for their old tried-and-true *Rockets*, which by then had clicked off some 4.3 million miles and carried 5 million passengers in safety and comfort. Within a few months, Rock Island banished the *Jet Rocket* to the 44-mile Chicago–Joliet commuter run, where it ran as the *Banker's Special*, the road's plushest commuter train. In the meantime, Union Pacific and New York Central had been trying out the *Aerotrains*. When they tired of the experiment, Rock Island picked up the two lightweights—cheaply—and pressed them into suburban service. Between the

lightweights, Fairbanks-Morse and Alco road switchers, BL2s, and a few other oddities, Rock Island had the strangest commuter fleet in North America.

Downhill Years

In 1957, for the first time ever, Rock Island was missing from *Trains* magazine's annual speed survey—none of its trains were running 70 miles per hour or more, except for a 71-mile dash on Fort Worth & Denver track in Texas.

Still, the road was not giving up easily. "I speak only for the Rock Island when I say that we're in the passenger business to stay," said Rock Island's new president, Downing B. Jenks. "I think we face a challenge that we can meet, and with some measure of success." If the road could no longer run fast, it could

Operating in push-pull mode, passenger F7A No. 676 backs a morning train of bi-levels toward La Salle Street in October 1972. Rising in the background, Sears Tower is a little over halfway to its full 108 stories and 1973 completion. *Paul C. Hunnell*

run cheap. In 1959 roundtrip first-class fares were cut 28 percent. Competing railroads grumbled, then cut their fares. Rock Island also let passengers ride in parlor cars for the price of a coach fare plus a special seat charge. By then, except for on the *Golden State*, the railroad had taken over operation of its sleepers from Pullman.

Ridership bounced back by 25 percent, and with it passenger revenues, by 12 percent. The fare reduction was extended. Strangely, when the Interstate Commerce Commission (ICC) proposed federal subsidies for "essential" passenger trains, Rock Island objected.

But, along with SP, the road also petitioned ICC—unsuccessfully—for permission to consolidate the *Golden State* with Trains 39 and 40, remnants of the old *Imperial*. The passenger business was losing $1 million a year by 1965. The road tried another round of fare reductions, cutting both first-class and coach tickets on all its *Rockets* by 25 percent Mondays through Thursdays. Passengers were unresponsive.

Commuterville

Rock Island's distinctive commuter trains were as much a part of the Windy City experience as the El or the Lakefront. Every weekday morning, tens of thousands of riders poured across the platforms of the venerable La Salle Street station, arriving from neighborhoods and bedroom communities scattered along the road's two suburban routes: the main line via Longwood and Robbins to Joliet, and the dedicated commuter line to Beverly Hills, Morgan Park, and Blue Island. Over the years, these commuters rode a bewildering variety of equipment behind an assortment of motive power that only a railfan could love.

The Rock's first suburban trains ran in 1865, nine years after Illinois Central's commuter service. Blue-painted "dummy" engines hauled riders to stops at 92nd and 95th streets, Chicago Junction, Blue Island, 103rd Street, and Vincennes. As the city grew, the service expanded, eventually reaching out to Oak Forest, Tinley Park, Mokena, and, by 1907, Joliet. Fares were cheap—a dime a ride, a 25-ride coupon for $2. And the road was making money—almost $600,000 a year by 1910.

Those early wooden coaches were lighted by gas and heated by coal stoves, a necessary fire hazard in frigid Chicago winters. Electric lighting and train heat came later with a fleet of small Forney 2-6-6 tank engines, which hustled the trains out to Blue Island in 45 to 50 minutes. The road's suburban lines served mostly middle-class neighborhoods where the upwardly mobile children of the old ethnic neighborhoods found homes and easy access to jobs in the Loop.

With arrival in the early 1920s of the first all-steel "Al Capone" coaches—named for the Chicago bootleg boss—the Forneys gave way to 2-6-0s, and eventually to Ten-Wheelers and lanky 4-4-2s bumped down from secondary mainline runs. Later, steel cars were equipped with roller bearings and double doors offset from the ends of the car for quicker loading and unloading. The Al Capones soldiered on until delivery of the first truly modern commuter coaches in 1949. With four double-wide sliding doors per car, air-conditioning in every other car, high-speed electric brakes, fabric-covered seats, and fold-down armrests, they represented the state of the art.

Meanwhile up front, 4-6-2 Pacifics replaced smaller engines, only to be themselves bumped by the first diesels—a pair of 1,500-horsepower Fairbanks-Morses and a fleet of 10 EMD FP-7s. Altogether, Rock Island spent $4 million on its commuter service in 1949. Alco boiler-equipped RS-3s began taking over in 1951.

More modern coaches arrived in 1953, and a decade later the Rock had its first bi-level push-pull coaches. The old steel Al Capones were retired to a scrap dealer. However, the time when any railroad could make money on commuters had long passed, and the Rock's suburban losses were running over $1 million a year. By the late 1970s, when the road was still running 77 daily suburban trains, it was seeking help from the federal and state governments.

Over the years, suburban service became the final

Piece by piece, train by train, the passenger business fell apart. Sleepers began to vanish from consists; diners were replaced by box lunches on many trains. The *Twin Star Rocket* was cut south of Fort Worth. Trains 39 and 40 were dropped, and the Rock petitioned to discontinue the *Rocky Mountain Rocket*, now coach-only. Instead, the train was cut back to Chicago–Omaha service and renamed the *Cornhusker*. The *Twin Star Rocket* was cut back again, to Kansas City, and renamed the *Plainsman*.

Rock Island's 1966 annual report sounded a faint note of optimism. "Although passenger revenues continued to decline in 1966 and are expected to drop further in 1967, the company has nevertheless taken steps to give service on the remaining trains that is as good as circumstances permit. Even though this is a highly deficit service, it is the company's one point of contact with a great many people, and Rock Island must give them as good an impression of the railroad as its financial condition allows."

Then in 1967, the U.S. Post Office

AB6 No. 750 has already made her inbound morning run and now, pausing to collect a few passengers at Englewood, is on her way to Joliet with a short suburban train on April 21, 1965. One of a unique twosome, the unit is really a cab-equipped E6B built in 1940 for the Colorado Springs section of the *Rocky Mountain Rocket. Marty Bernard*

assignment for an odd-lot assortment of Rock Island passenger power: early E-units, FP-7s, the road's two unique A-B units built for *Rocky Mountain Rocket* service, secondhand Union Pacific E8s, and even the three low-riding experimental trains, the *Jet Rocket* and GM *Aerotrains*. Passengers may not have been impressed, but camera-toting railfans gathered on the Roosevelt Road overpass to record the passing show.

In 1977, as it became apparent Rock Island would

not survive into the next decade, the road signed an agreement with the Chicago Regional Transportation Authority (CRTA), essentially turning over its commuter service. CRTA bought new locomotives, new coaches, and rehabilitated 6.6 miles of track. The ancient La Salle Street station was razed, its place taken by a new high-rise. There, at ground level, Metra's gleaming trains still arrive from and depart to the old stops.

Tucked away under the shadow of the El, the entrance to the La Salle Street station nevertheless is a familiar sight to Chicagoland commuters. At 3:30 p.m. on March 20, 1975, the afternoon rush has not begun, and the concourse is silent. But upstairs in the company's headquarters, officers are busy, grappling with merger proposals and the implications of bankruptcy. *Bill Marvel*

eliminated all RPOs from America's railroads. Jervis Langdon Jr., who had become president of the road in 1965, warned in the employee magazine that loss of the mail would cost Rock Island $1 million in revenues. By the end of the year, Rock and SP were asking ICC for permission to drop the *Golden State*, which was losing $500,000 a year, as well as Memphis–Tucumcari Trains 21 and 22 and the *Peoria Rocket*. The *Golden State* ran its last mile on February 21, 1968. Only seven cars were tied behind the three E-units. There were 88 passengers on board, barely enough fill half the seats on one the Boeing 707s that had been flying the Los Angeles route for 10 years.

In 1969 Rock Island quietly dropped the *Rocket* name from its timetables. Even

Railfans seldom bothered to photograph the "other" end of push-pull suburban runs. But at New Lenox on January 30, 1977, the camera has focused on Pullman-Standard bi-level cab car CC116 as an E-unit shoves it toward La Salle Street. *Kevin Piper*

the Peoria train, the core of its business, was now just the *Peorian*. In a further blow to Rock heritage, Langdon proposed to move the remaining passenger trains out of La Salle Street and into bland Chicago Union Station—a move that never came about.

By summer 1970, the two daily Chicago–Rock Island and four Peoria trains were the only passenger services left outside the commuter zone. Surprisingly, each still offered a diner and a club-lounge. The Illinois legislature in 1973 voted a $1.5 million subsidy for the six remaining intercity trains. As Amtrak took over most of the nation's intercity passenger trains, Rock Island could not afford the price of entry—a sum equal to the road's 1969 passenger losses—and opted instead to

E7As Nos. 639 and 641 are running on borrowed time on July 7, 1977, as they hustle suburban train No. 423 through Blue Island. All but one of their nine sisters have been traded to EMD on new Geeps or ex-UP E9s. *Paul C. Hunnell*

keep operating its own Peoria and Rock Island trains.

Patronage on the Peoria train continued to decline, but the Rock Island held firm. The state approved a 15 percent fare increase and continued its subsidy. Even so, passenger trains were losing $2 million a year.

Rock Island passenger service thus ended where it began, with trains to Peoria and Rock Island. They rolled on into 1979 still losing money. But by then Rock Island had much, much bigger problems.

CHAPTER SIX

THE ROAD TO RUIN

By the late 1950s the signs were not good for the railroad business. The prosperity that had returned with World War II had largely dissipated. Jet airliners were scooping up the high-end passenger trade, and the growing interstate highway system would soon harvest what was left. Freight was going to trucks and barges. A railroad president in 1956 had to be on his toes, especially the president of a railroad with the systemic problems of Rock Island.

Most of what was wrong with the Rock went back to the beginning. Everywhere it went, some other railroad got there first

Bad-order cars and engines have begun to accumulate from all over the system, and Silvis is a scene of desolation by August 4, 1979. Even though freight is still moving, the end is near for Rock Island. GP38-2 Nos. 4477 and 4473, foreground, will be sold to Grand Trunk Western, and GP40 No. 4716, just beyond, will be reclaimed by owner and leaser Union Pacific. National Railway Equipment, a used-locomotive dealer, will take over operation of Silvis shops. *Ed Seay Jr.*

The wheat harvest has been gathered, and on August 17, 1958, No. 9011 rests under the cottonwoods at Phillipsburg, Kansas. Not a doodlebug, but a boxcab freight engine, No. 9011 was one of seven turned out in 1929 by St. Louis Car Company. *Tom Lee photo, Tom Klinger collection*

and went there more directly. And when Rock Island did get there, it was over somebody else's tracks.

Rock was a granger road, with everything that implied. Dependent upon shipments of Midwestern corn and wheat, it was also dependent upon Midwestern seasons and weather. Droughts, bad crop years, and floods affected it more than other, more diversified railroads. Rock Island had little of the coal traffic that plumped Burlington's bottom line. The big manufacturing enterprises of the East thinned out west of the Quad Cities on the Illinois-Iowa border. Consequently, only the 200 miles between Chicago and the Mississippi were heavily used. The rest of its

lines were thinly traveled. Bridge traffic went to faster competitors. The Rock lacked what Richard Saunders Jr., in *Merging Lines*, called "geographic integrity." It ran all the way up into South Dakota and deep down into Louisiana. It could claim only the Golden State Route as truly its own. And west of Kansas City, that country was mostly empty.

Downing B. Jenks, who became Rock Island president at the end of 1955, was well aware of Rock's problems. Far-sighted and a believer in cooperation between railroads, Jenks realized that the road's only salvation lay in merger with a stronger partner. In 1959 Jenks quietly entered discussions with the 10,592-mile Milwaukee Road. The two lines hired consulting engineers Coverdale & Colpitts to study the operational possibilities and railroad investment specialists R. W.

A rare visitor down South, BL2 No. 429 leads an FB-1 and a GP7 through Dallas in one of those only-on-the-Rock motive power assortments that left local railfans grateful. It's the late 1950s, and this 1949-built unit still wears its original red and black colors. *E. L. DeGolyer Jr. photo, Ed Seay Jr. collection*

Well into the 1950s, passengers could ride an unscheduled mixed train on certain Iowa and Arkansas branch lines. Spartan accommodations were provided in 20 passenger-baggage cabooses converted from outside-braced boxcars before World War II. In June 1959, the No. 17778 and a companion have just emerged from the Cedar Rapids paint shop. *Lloyd Keyser*

Still wearing the "Route of the ROCKETS" slogan and its original red-and-black paint with white wings, GP7 No. 1298 idles in Peach Yard, Fort Worth, sometime in the early 1960s. Sister No. 1250, just behind, has recently been repainted in a new maroon-and-pinstripe scheme. *L. Ackerman photo, Ed Seay Jr. collection*

Pressprich & Company to study the financial consequences of a merger. However, in 1961 Jenks was lured away to the Missouri Pacific, ending merger discussions. Almost immediately Chicago & North Western began talks with the Milwaukee. North Western's Ben Heineman had in mind a three-way marriage of North Western, Milwaukee, and the Rock.

With Jenks' departure, John Farrington, now 70, briefly resumed the presidency.

When Farrington died in late 1961, R. Ellis Johnson became president.

A merger seemed Rock Island's best long-range hope. In the meantime, there was a railroad to run. Only so much could be done to arrest the slow-motion collapse of the passenger business, and Rock Island was doing most of it. Freight prospects were brighter. The business of hauling trailers on railroad flatcars seemed poised to take some lucrative freight business back from long-haul truckers. The question was how to go about this.

Farrington, with his enthusiasm for ultra-lightweight passenger trains, saw an opportunity in a new technology devised by

ACF, builder of the *Jet Rocket*. Called Adapto, the system replaced the truck trailer with a detachable container that could be lifted from a truck bed and placed on a specially designed four-wheel, air-cushioned flatcar, saving considerable weight. In 1956, Rock Island bought into the system, acquiring 50 Adapto flats and 90 containers and launching "Covert-A-Frate" service between major terminals.

Rock Island's vice president John W. Barriger III was looking far beyond Adapto, and far beyond mergers to the future of the entire railroad industry. Former president of Monon, Barriger had been thinking big since the 1930s, when he studied Rock Island's route across Iowa and proposed a whole new 160-mile high-speed, high-density line. Now,

he had something bigger in mind: creation of what he called a "Super Railroad." Such an entity would gather up 40,000 of the most strategic railroad miles and rebuild them for 160-car, 70-mile-per-hour freights and 1,000-seat, 100-mile-per-hour streamliners. There would be no grades over 0.5 percent (1 percent in mountains); 300 miles of new tunnels, including a dozen double-tracked super tunnels; and 4,000 miles of line relocations. Yards would be modernized or

continued on page 140

Red boxcars and maroon geeps—in April 1964, things appear as unchanging as the Texas horizon, as GP7 No. 1300 and two sisters idle in the Fort Worth yard. However, Union Pacific and Chicago & North Western have already begun the long battle to control the railroad—the battle that many will later consider the beginning of the end for Rock Island. *Lloyd Keyser*

In February 1964, Alco FA-1 No. 131 awaits a crew change in Herington, Kansas, where the line splits for Tucumcari and Fort Worth. Though re-engined by EMD in 1954, the Alco freighters were never popular with Rock Island crews or shop workers. *Ron Hill*

Always the Chicago hangout for visiting railfans, the Roosevelt Road viaduct always offered some curiosity. Here, on May 13, 1964, it's a rear view of BL2 No. 427, an engine that, from this angle, looks more automotive than locomotive. *Marty Bernard*

continued from page 137

abandoned. Thousands of high-horsepower diesels would be added to the fleet, along with hundreds of thousands of high-capacity freight cars. Total cost: $20 billion.

It was bold and visionary, and it wasn't going to happen, not with the way railroads were regulated and capitalized. In 1956, Barriger left Rock Island to take up presidency of the Pittsburgh & Lake Erie. One of the most farseeing railroad thinkers of his time, he later reappeared in the Rock Island story, near the bitter end.

Merger Madness

In June 1962, Ellis Johnson announced that he had spent a week with Southern Pacific's Donald Russell, talking merger. They seemed like natural partners: Rock Island– SP's Golden State Route had prospered since the early 1900s, enriched by seasonal flows of California produce. In September, UP joined in the talks. A UP–Rock Island combination made even more sense. UP would gain coveted access to Chicago and St. Louis; the Golden State Route and all lines south of Kansas City would go to SP. Everyone would win. Rock Island stock climbed from $20 to $26 a share.

The following summer, UP put its proposal on the table. Rock Island's board recommended stockholders accept the offer.

With a UP–Rock Island combination suddenly threatening Chicago & North Western's Omaha connections, Ben Heineman moved quickly. His railroad made a counteroffer and filed its own plan with the Interstate Commerce Commission (ICC), calling for the Chicago & North Western–

Milwaukee Road–Rock Island combination. Alarmed, Santa Fe and Missouri Pacific announced that *they* were talking merger and invited interested western railroads to join them.

Heineman's action put the UP–Rock Island merger on a side track.

In late 1964, Jervis Langdon Jr. was elected Rock Island chairman and CEO. Fresh from nursing Baltimore & Ohio back to financial health, Langdon would spend most of his career on troubled railroads. He was UP's man, brought in to smooth the tracks to a merger.

However, the opposition was lining up: Milwaukee, Rio Grande, Missouri Pacific, and Western Pacific (which ran nowhere near Rock Island territory) all challenged the merger. In reply UP distributed a slick, color brochure arguing its case. With two offers to consider, the Rock's stockholders waffled, failing to give UP the needed majority. A federal judge ordered another vote, and UP upped the ante, promising to pour $200 million into Rock's decaying physical plant. At the moment, UP was worth $1.7 billion. Rock Island assets were $497 million. This time stockholders overwhelmingly voted approval.

With UP money available, the road began buying Electro-Motive GP35s and

Resplendent in maroon and stainless steel, E6A No. 630 brings a touch of elegance to commuter service in April 1965 as it clatters across the Pennsylvania diamonds at Englewood. This prewar unit will survive as the last of her kind. *Marty Bernard*

General Electric U25Bs, its first modern power in years, and much needed freight cars. The new locomotives soon found work on the *Gemini*, a joint Rock Island–New York Central hotshot running all the way from Silvis to Elkhart, Indiana, bypassing congested Chicago. Rock Island and SP also pooled power between Chicago and Los Angeles.

Rio Grande challenged the merger, announcing that as a condition it wanted Rock Island's lines to the Missouri River and trackage rights almost everywhere on SP. Heineman, meanwhile, pushed the ICC to require that Rock Island sell everything south of Herington, Kansas, to Santa Fe, while the Santa Fe proposed splitting the Rock with North Western. Missouri Pacific, which was buying up Santa Fe stock, asked the commission to bundle all petitions and counter-petitions into one giant merger

It's been 10 days since floods took out Union Pacific's Limon–Denver line, Rock Island's usual route into the Mile High City, so on June 27, 1965, GP9 No. 1314 struggles up the hill to Palmer Lake on Santa Fe–Rio Grande's Joint Line with a detour train of piggybacks. *Bill Marvel*

case. Soo Line also wanted all merger cases consolidated.

Perhaps in relief, UP, SP, and Rock Island assented. The ICC now faced the most complicated railroad consolidation case in its history. Proceedings rolled on through 1967 and into 1968. For three years in a row, the Rock lost money—$17.9 million in 1967 alone—its situation now desperate. Speaking at Texas A&M, an exasperated Jervis Langdon

complained that the merger case now took up 43,000 pages of testimony, most of it arcane arguments over who might lose traffic to whom. The United States had too many railroads, anyway, Langdon told his audience, too many junctions and interchanges and delays. What was needed, he said, was "fewer railroads—far fewer." Ultimately, he said, "one railroad for the entire United States." It sounded like Barriger's Super Railroad. If the

Just coming up on the Kansas River Bridge at Manhattan, GP18 No. 1334 slows with 20-car freight No. 73 for Belleville and points west on November 7, 1965. Across the river, the train will pause, bump across the UP tracks, skirt the south edge of town, and meet its eastbound counterpart, No. 74. *Tom Lee photo, Tom Klinger collection*

railroads couldn't figure out how to do it, he said, the ICC should make them.

Nineteen sixty-nine came and went. The Rock cut its rates on grain shipments by 25 percent and experimented with unit grain trains that were almost as long as those ICC proceedings—in one case, 201 cars behind 10 locomotives on a quick turnaround between Enid and the port of Galveston. In an effort to make sense of the Midwestern rail situation, the U.S. Department of Transportation proposed consolidation into three regional mega-railroads. Nobody paid attention.

The Rock repainted its engines maroon with yellow noses, but fresh paint couldn't cover its underlying condition. The road was getting less than 10 percent of the cars handed over by UP at Council Bluffs. The truth was, its tracks were in no shape to handle more.

Then, just when Rock Island seemed to need him most, Jervis Langdon was appointed a trustee for bankrupt Penn Central. William Dixon took his place. As the ICC machinery ground inexorably onward—the transcript now ran to 155,000 pages—more trouble

arose: In response to galloping inflation, President Richard Nixon had imposed a price and wage freeze in August 1971. Railroad workers were due a wage increase by that October. If it were made retroactive to the start of the freeze, Dixon warned employees, their railroad would be crippled.

He pleaded with them in the pages of *The Rocket*: Rock Island is respected, he said, "because those who use its services know that everyone associated with it is anxious to do a job. If we are to continue to maintain that position in the forefront of the transportation industry, we must be more willing, more accommodating, more diligent, more concerned, and more knowledgeable than the next fellow."

Those willing employees struggled through the winter of 1972–1973, when a spring blizzard blocked the Colorado line for five days. By summer only two of the road's freights were running faster than 55 miles per hour, both on the Golden State Route. The fall brought a rush of business as the United

continued on page 148

Taller than an ordinary NW1, 1938 EMC product No. 701 putters around Kelly Yard at Silvis, powered by a derated Alco 12-244 engine from an FA freighter that, in turn, received an EMD prime mover. In March 1966, the rare hybrid has only nine more months of work ahead of it before going in to EMD on a trade-in. *Terry Norton*

Whitcomb 75-ton switcher No. 1009 rests in the Silvis dead line in September 1967, at the end of a long and very eventful career. Built in 1949 by Whitcomb and Canadian Locomotive Company for Canadian National branch-line service, 17 of the switchers were sold to Rock Island, re-engined, and put to work for which they were underpowered and ill-suited. Nevertheless, most lasted into the 1960s, when they were—gratefully— traded to GE or EMD. *Bill Marvel*

Overleaf: Almost all that remains of Rock Island's long-haul passenger service by May 1968, the Kansas City–Minneapolis *Plainsman* hustles by Hardesty Avenue on its last lap to Kansas City Union Station. *Ron Hill*

Rio Grande's North Yard played host to Rock Island freight power in the diesel era, which explains 1946-built F2A No. 47 sharing the service tracks with much younger Rio Grande GP30 No. 3019. By February 5, 1969, the date of this photo, most of the Grande's own freight F-units were stored or traded in to EMD on newer power. *Neil Shankweiler photo, Tom Klinger collection*

continued from page 144
States began exporting grain to the Soviet Union. Burdened by this windfall, the power-short Rock leased units wherever it could find them. Railfans gathered at trackside to watch the colorful parade of Chesapeake & Ohio and Western Maryland GP9s, Detroit Edison SD40s and U30Cs, U28Bs from Pittsburgh & Lake Erie, and a lone Belt Railway of Chicago GP9. The Rock traded 31 worn-out F7s to UP for 31 of that road's F9s, and 10 additional units went to Rio Grande in exchange for Geeps. The Rock then ordered 18 new U30s and 12 GP40-2s.

Cash-starved, the following year the road sold 80 GP7s and GP9s to Precision National Leasing, which sent them to Morrison-Knudsen for rebuilding, then leased them back to the Rock. John Ingram, who had made a name for himself in marketing and sales at New York Central and Illinois Central, was brought in as president. In 10 years the road had not turned a profit, and the country was entering a recession. The desperate board turned to on-line shippers for cash and pleaded for a $100 million rehabilitation loan from the United States Railroad Administration (USRA).

Pieces of the Rock

On November 8, 1974, after 11 years, 300 lawyers, and more than 200,000 pages of transcripts, the ICC gave conditional approval to the UP–Rock Island merger. The conditions: Rio Grande would get the line to Omaha. Everything south of Kansas City would go to SP. Santa Fe could have the old Choctaw Route to Memphis. Jobs would be protected, and some existing traffic arrangements would be preserved.

In the end, the list of conditions proved unacceptable to Union Pacific—that and Rock Island's physical shape, which was too far gone to be of use to UP. The USRA loaned the road $9 million, less than a tenth of what it had asked. Another request, for a $30 million "emergency" loan, was turned down. In March 1975, Rock Island entered bankruptcy for the third and last time.

The final years tested Ingram's marketing know-how. Like Farrington before him, the road's new president set about creating a new,

Ten C415s were the final order of switchers purchased by Rock Island and the last active Alcos on the property. Three of the tribe—Nos. 420, 418, and 416—congregate on New Year's Day, 1972 at Blue Island, home base for the oddball units since they were purchased in 1966. *Paul C. Hunnell*

more positive image. Boxcars were painted bright white and blue, lettered simply "The Rock." The legendary John W. Barriger returned as "senior traveling freight agent," a sort of super-salesman, crisscrossing the road in his private car, drumming up business.

But Rock Island's troubles went beyond marketing. Creditors wanted the road broken up, the pieces sold off. Federal Judge Frank McGarr, playing for time, granted the road permission to lease 56 new GP38-2s for an optimistic 15 years. The units emerged from Electro-Motive Division in the new blue-and-white image, each named in honor of an on-line community or "friend" of the railroad (No. 4310 became *The American Railfan*).

Meanwhile, Ingram cut costs. Workers were furloughed, executive offices emptied. Train speeds were lowered. Ingram proposed that all lines not essential to Rock Island's agricultural mission be sold or abandoned. His most radical proposal was for the Rock and other Midwest grain-haulers to band together, sharing tracks, yards, rolling stock, sales staff, and payroll. Dubbed "FarmRail"— or "Conrail West" by its critics, the enterprise would radio-dispatch trains when and where

needed, with two-man crews.

The plan, which prefigured today's regional railroads, was ahead of its time. And time was running out for Rock Island. Though traffic was starting to increase, with new diesels at work and track crews busy laying welded rail on new ties, the USRA still refused further loans (even though SP had offered $57 million for the Golden State Route). "We can't wait forever," Judge McGarr warned Ingram. A new deadline for a bankruptcy plan was set for January 1979, then extended six months. And extended again.

Just when it seemed the agony would drag on forever, the Brotherhood of Railway and Airline Clerks announced a strike against the Rock Island for retroactive wages. Judge McGarr warned a strike would be, literally, the end of the road.

It was, in many ways, a mercy killing. By
continued on page 152

Overleaf: Power-starved Rock Island in early 1972 picked up 19 F9AM units from Union Pacific. Already worn out, most of them managed to hang on for several years until traded to EMD for a batch of UP-owned GP38-2s. In November 1972, No. 4157 creeps around the north edge of Denver on the Sandown Cutoff with Train 82 for Blue Island. *Ron Hill*

continued from page 149

August, when the workers finally walked out, SP was warning that the long-prized Golden State Route was almost beyond salvaging. The following month, ICC ordered Kansas City Terminal Railway to take over and run Rock Island at government expense for the next 60 days. Estimated cost: $457 a car. The commission invited SP to bid on the Golden State Route. On Friday afternoon, January 25, 1980, Judge McGarr ruled that the Rock was beyond saving. He ordered trustee William Gibbons to shut down operations after March 23 and prepare for liquidation.

When the end came, everyone, it seemed, wanted a piece of the Rock. Other railroads submitted 17 bids that, taken together, accounted for 65 percent of its trackage and 85 percent of its traffic. It was the largest

bankruptcy liquidation in U.S. history up until that time. Chicago & North Western bid on the Twin Cities–Kansas City main. The Missouri-Kansas-Texas wanted the line from Herington to Fort Worth. Reaching out of its accustomed territory, Grand Trunk Western bid on the Chicago–Council Bluffs and Des Moines–Kansas City lines, plus the Peoria branch. SP still wanted the Santa Rosa–St. Louis line, and Missouri Pacific bid for Memphis–Little Rock.

Kansas City Terminal had already begun shutting off shipments for points on the Rock Island. The last official train ran March 31, though for weeks afterward lone engines could be seen dragging rows of stranded cars down weed-grown tracks. In this way equipment and rolling stock

continued on page 157

Massive wheat shipments to the Soviet Union sent Rock Island scrambling for motive power, which explains the leased Detroit Edison U30C behind U28B No. 253. The train is crossing the Des Plaines River bridge on the final stretch to Burr Oak Yard on May 26, 1973.
Ed Kanak

Trading speed for power, U33B Nos. 297 and 290 have been re-geared to operate with road slug No. 284, a cut-down U25B without a prime mover. Shown preparing to depart Blue Island on June 4, 1977, the U33Bs provide extra tractive effort to the slug. Five such combinations roam the system.
Paul C. Hunnell

In January 1978, Rock Island and Braniff International are playing out the string. The railroad will vanish in 1980, the airline in 1982. GP38 No. 4305 is arriving at Sandown Junction outside of Denver; the Boeing 727 in the distance is taking off from Stapleton Airport. *Ron Hill*

It's December 1978, and bankrupt Rock Island is awaiting a Union Pacific merger that will never come. But there is still work to be done as GP40 No. 376 and SW No. 523 pair up on a transfer drag along St. Paul Bluffs, bound from Inver Grove Yard to Burlington Northern in the Twin Cities. *Ed Kanak*

It's June 6, 1980, and Rock Island has run its last. But here at Maplewood, Missouri, the Rock lives on briefly as a perfect set of GP38-2s haul freight for new owner, Missouri Pacific. Named the *David P. Morgan* for the longtime *Trains* magazine editor, No. 4315 will soon be renumbered into MoPac's roster. *Mike Woodruff*

The herald on the nose is familiar, and the restored Chillicothe, Illinois, station looks better than ever. But ES44AC No. 503 belongs to the 500-mile Iowa Interstate, a regional that continues to perform valuable service on former Rock Island trackage. On February 13, 2009, in the company of two GP38-2s and another ES44AC, the unit is on its way down the Peoria line to pick up coal for Cedar Rapids, Iowa. *Steve Smedley*

continued from page 152

was gathered up and sold. The liquidation raised $500 million, probably more than Rock Island was worth as a going railroad. The corporate skeleton lived on as a holding company, Chicago Pacific Corporation. In 1985 it was sold to Maytag, the washing-machine folks.

Afterward, there were reminders if you knew where to look: a rusting Pacific-type locomotive in a park, a vintage diesel in a legacy paint scheme, here and there a fading emblem on an overpass. But few bothered to look.

Still, Rock Island was no Rio Grande Southern, no New York, Ontario & Western, vanishing abruptly without a trace, rails taken up, weeds invading the abandoned right-of-way. It speaks to the wisdom of its founders that so much of its track survives.

In the end, nobody wanted the old Choctaw Route. The long, scenic line from

Rock Island passenger colors adorn Iowa Northern F40PHR No. 678 at Cedar Rapids on August 25, 2007, with a *Hawkeye Express* excursion headed for Iowa City on Cedar Rapids & Iowa City rails. Iowa Northern operates 163 miles, mostly over one-time Rock Island branches. *Tom McNair*

Kansas City to St. Louis is gone. However, the Golden State Route has come roaring back to life under UP. UP also runs up to the Twin Cities and down into Texas. Iowa Interstate, a strong regional carrier, operates the entire Chicago–Omaha line and proudly carries Rock Island's herald on the nose of its diesels. Another regional, Kyle, crosses the high plains to Limon, though not to Denver or Colorado Springs.

And the Rock has entered folklore, remembered in a traditional American blues/folk song first recorded in the 1930s by Huddie William "Leadbelly" Ledbetter and later by Johnny Cash, among others:

The Rock Island Line is a mighty good road
The Rock Island Line is the road to ride
The Rock Island Line is a mighty good road
If you want to ride you gotta ride it like you find it
Get your ticket at the station for the Rock Island Line

Epilogue: Pieces of the Rock

More than three decades after its death, the railroad that Union Pacific President John C. Kenefick once called "a bag of bones" remains a pretty lively skeleton. An arm or leg might be missing, but thousands of former Rock Island rail miles still get regular exercise.

Most of the old Memphis-Tucumcari Choctaw Route has gone to weeds with the exception of a 74-mile Oklahoma segment operated since 1996 by Arkansas-Oklahoma, which, incidentally, decorates the nose of its red and yellow diesels with the familiar Rock Island herald.

The 57-mile Fordyce & Princeton and the 26.2-mile Ouachita Railroad operate two segments of Rock Island's otherwise silent Arkansas and Louisiana lines.

The Kansas City–St. Louis line is being reclaimed by nature and by hikers. Only a few miles from Vigus to Pleasant Hill, Missouri, survive as the Missouri Central. Out on the rolling high plains of Western Kansas and Eastern Colorado, Rail America's Kyle Railroad hauls grain and roofing material over the route of the Rocky Mountain Rocket. Kyle's trains begin their trek in Belleville but stop well short of Denver and Colorado Springs in Limon, site of the old Limon do-si-do. Denver Rock Island, a switching road, serves a few miles of Rock Island trackage on the northern fringe of Denver.

Two pieces of the Rock survive in Texas and Oklahoma, the Texas & Northwestern from Etter to Pringle, and the Wichita, Tillman & Jackson, from Waurika to Walters.

Another regional, Iowa Northern, took over Rock Island's 163-mile Cedar Falls-Manly, Iowa, line in 1984 and survived a catastrophic flood in 2008 to cash in on the growing ethanol business.

For every mile given over to weeds or to regionals, other miles of Rock Island thrive as busy main-line railroad. As more than one person has observed, in the end Kenefick's Union Pacific wound up with a far bigger share of Rock Island than it had ever contemplated in 1962 when it began its campaign to acquire several strategic pieces of the railroad. Under the UP banner, the Golden State Route—always a vital link in the California-Chicago flow of goods and seasonal produce, and now container traffic, is humming as never before.

Mighty UP's 1995 purchase of Chicago & North Western brought with it RI's coveted Twin City–Kansas City "spine." Combined with its former Missouri Pacific lines, UP now enjoys an uninterrupted haul from the upper Midwest to the ports of Houston and Galveston. Acquisition of MoPac also brought to UP Rock Island's Fort Worth–Herrington, Kansas, conveyor of gain and crushed rock.

In 1988 when it looked as if C&NW might remain independent or fall to another carrier, depriving UP of its longed-for Chicago connection, Kenefick's road made a bid to buy Rock Island's original 533-mile Blue Island, Illinois, to Council Bluffs main line. The line plus the historic Bureau-Peoria branch was already being operated—and still is—by 1984 start-up Iowa Interstate. (From Blue Island on into Chicago, IAIS runs on Metra, Chicago region's suburban rail system.)

Today four Iowa Interstate freights cross Illinois and Iowa between Blue Island and Council Bluffs each day, pumping new life through the heart of the old Rock Island.

If some railfans standing along the Council Bluffs line in the early 1960s were transposed through time to 2012, they might be mildly surprised at the locomotive rumbling by—engine 513, a 2009-built GE ES44AC. But the red-and-black paint scheme and the maroon nose shield would be completely familiar: Rock Island, doing business as usual.

Iowa Interstate has done more than bring life back to rails many thought were dead. IAIS also is keeping the memory of Rock Island alive with the 513 and its "heritage" paint scheme and with the rest of its 47-unit diesel fleet. Painted in striking red and black with yellow trim, all proudly carry their road name within the Rock Island shield, an "historical homage to our predecessor line," says J. P. Lipka, the road's president and CEO. Best of all, perhaps, a pair of Chinese-built QJ 2-10-2 steam locomotives wear the historic emblem on their tanks. Acquired in 2006 and "Americanized" in appearance in 2011, they are fired up every now and then to storm across Illinois and Iowa with an excursion or a freight train, reminders of an even older Rock Island.

NOTES

1. The Bridge

Rock Island's origin and earliest years are summarized by the road itself for the benefit of new employees in a "Yard Clerical Manual." Material from the 1970 edition can be found online at http://www.rits.org/www/histories/RIHistory.html.

A "Rock Island's Family Tree," compiled by Matt Willett, at http://home.covad.net/~scicoatnsew/rihist1.htm, lists by year the incorporation and construction of Rock Island's component parts.

The Rock Island story from its founding to arrival at the Missouri River appears in William Edward Hayes' *Iron Road to Empire: The History of 100 Years of the Progress and Achievements of the Rock Island Lines* (New York: Simons-Boardman, 1953), pp. 3–67.

A Most Magnificent Machine: America Adopts the Railroad, 1825–1862, by Craig Miner (Lawrence: University of Kansas Press, 2010), pp. 188–189, recounts the excursion and celebration marking Rock Island's 1854 arrival at its namesake city.

Frank P. Donovan's *Iowa Railroads* (Iowa City: University of Iowa Press, 2000), pp. 168–174, and Don L. Hofsommer's *Steel Trails of Hawkeye Land* (Bloomington: Indiana University Press, 2005), pp. 2–18, follow the road's progress, or lack thereof, from the Mississippi to the Missouri Rivers.

Henry Farnam's role is the subject of Alvin F. Harlow's "Farnam Built the Rock Island," *Trains* 9, no. 2 (December 1948), pp. 42–51. Accounts of the remarkable career of John Bloomfield Jervis appear in "John Bloomfield Jervis," by John R. Spears, *Bulletin No. 30* (February 1933), of the Railway and Locomotive Historical Society, pp. 5–29, and in "Jervis, John B. (1795–1885)," by William D. Middleton, in the *Encyclopedia of North American Railroads,* p. 568.

The Quad Cities website (http://www.qconline.com/rilines2004) contains the early history of the railroad, including a chronology, an account of that first meeting with Colonel George Davenport, biographies of Henry Farnam and Joseph Sheffield, and quotes from contemporary speeches and newspaper accounts.

Abe Lincoln for the Defense

For Abraham Lincoln's efforts on behalf of railroads generally and the Rock Island in particular, see John W. Starr's *Lincoln and the Railroads: A Biographical Study* (New York: Dodd, Mead, and Co., 1927); for the Bridge case, see pp. 92–116. Shorter accounts can be found in "Lincoln and the Railroads," *Trains* 6, no. 4 (February 1946), pp. 41–44, and in "Abraham Lincoln (1809–1865)," by Peter A. Hansen, *Encyclopedia of North American Railroads,* p. 159. The story of the Mississippi River Bridge and the resulting legal fallout is covered in "Bridging the Mississippi: The Railroads and Steamboats Clash at the Rock Island Bridge," by David A. Pfeiffer, a publication of the U.S. National Archives & Records Administration (vol. 36, no. 2, summer 2004) available at http://www.archives.gov/publications. Other accounts are in Hayes, *Iron Road to Empire,* pp. 47–49, and in Donovan, *Iowa Railroads,* pp. 171–173. The *Daily Press of Chicago,* on September 24, 1857, covered the lengthy arguments in *Hurd et al. vs. Railroad Bridge Co.* See also James W. Ely Jr.'s excellent article, "Lincoln and the Rock Island Bridge Case," at www.indianahistory.org.

Rock Island's historic crossing of the Mississippi is chronicled in "The Original Rock Island Bridge across the Mississippi River," by Frank F. Fowle, *Bulletin No. 56* (October 1941) of the Railway and Locomotive Historical Society, pp. 55–63. An extensive collection of pictures and maps of all the railroad's Mississippi bridges can be found at http://riveraction.org/node/121.

2. A Bend in the Road

Rock Island's push through Nebraska, Kansas, Missouri, Colorado, and Oklahoma to the Texas border, and the career of Ransom Cable, whom Grenville Dodge called "the most active and aggressive man west of Chicago," are covered in Hayes, *Iron Road to Empire,* pp. 56–151. Maury Klein's magisterial *Union Pacific: Birth of a Railroad, 1862–1893* (New York: Doubleday, 1987) recounts that transcontinental's efforts to control traffic and thwart Rock Island's westward progress, and Rock's counter-strategies. One response to UP pressure, the Iowa Pool, is covered in Hofsommer, *Steel Trails of Hawkeyland,* pp. 47–50.

Construction of Rock's line across southeastern Iowa to Missouri and beyond and further constructions and acquisitions in Iowa are covered in Donovan, *Iowa Railroads,* pp. 175–188, and Hofsommer's *Steel Trails of Hawkeyeland,* pp. 20–61. Rock Island's history in Oklahoma receives extensive attention in "The Railroads of Oklahoma," by Preston George and Sylvan R. Wood, *Bulletin No. 60* (January 1943) of the Railway and Locomotive Historical Society. For Colorado, see *The Chicago, Kansas and Nebraska Railway Came to Colorado,* by P. T. "Bob" Griswold (spiral-bound) (Brighton, Colo.: Sherm Conners Publishing, 2007).

For the 1871 Chicago Fire and its effects on the Rock Island, see Frank J. Nevins' "The LaSalle Street Station, Chicago, Illinois," *Bulletin No. 50* (October 1939) of the Railway and Locomotive Historical Society, pp. 5–29.

The Great Train Robbery

The James Gang encounter with Train Number 2 has long since entered folklore. For more authoritative accounts, consult Donald L. Gilmore's "When the James Gang Ruled the Rails," online at http://www.historynet.com/magazines/wild_west/3025691.html, and John Baskin Harper's "Jesse James Robbery of CRI&P at Adair, IA, Monday, July 21, 1873," the Rock Island Technical Society's *Digest* 19 (1999), pp. 54–80. T. J. Stiles' *Jesse James: Last Rebel of the Civil War* (New York: Knopf, 2007) provides a useful history of the outlaw's life and work.

3. A Rocky Road

Carl Snyder's *American Railways as Investments* (New York: Moody Corp., 1907) provides a fascinating snapshot of Rock Island's financial health and prospects as the twentieth century began.

The Reed-Moore Syndicate's depredations and the resulting bankruptcy are covered in Hayes, *Iron Road to Empire,* pp. 147–198. For a brief but telling summary, see "Rock Island Revived," *Fortune* 30, no. 6 (December 1944), pp. 219–220. The *New York Times* gave the "Rock Island fiasco" front-page coverage in its June 6 and August 18, 1915, editions.

David Myrick's *New Mexico's Railroads: An Historical Survey* (Golden: Colorado Railroad Museum, 1970), pp. 67–72 and 120–122, covers the push to Santa Rosa, New Mexico. For the Choctaw Route, see Hofsommer's *Railroads in Oklahoma* (Oklahoma City: Oklahoma Historical Society, 1977) and "The Railroads of Oklahoma," by Preston George and Sylvan R. Wood, *Bulletin No. 60* (January 1943) of the Railway and Locomotive Historical Society, esp. pp. 12–17, 23, 24, 41–44.

"U.S. Railroad Administration," by George M. Smerk, *Encyclopedia of North American Railroads,* pp. 1071–1076, offers a summary history of the railroads under federal administration.

4. Planned Progress

John Dow Farrington's transformation of the Rock Island into a modern railroad occupies pp. 233–295 in Hayes, *Iron Road to Empire;* see also "Rock Island Revived," *Fortune* 30, no. 6 (December 1944), pp. 140–148, 218–226. An example of Farrington's ability to motivate the rank-and-file is discussed in Hugh Hawkins' *Railwayman's Son: A Plains Family Memoir* (Lubbock: Texas Tech University Press, 2006), p. 70. Rock Island's survival and revival are celebrated in special centennial editions of trade publications, *Modern Railroads* 7, no. 10 (October 1952), and *Railway Age* 133, no. 14 (October 6, 1952).

"War Trains of the Rock Island," chapter 17, of S. Kip Farrington Jr.'s *Railroads at War* (New York: Coward-McCann, Inc., 1944), pp. 194–203, visits a wartime railroad as it labors to move men and material.

See *Trains and Travel* 12, no. 2 (December 1951), pp. 14–15, for a graphic account of the devastating 1951 Kansas River flood.

4–8–4s a-Plenty

A capsule roster of Rock Island steam power can be found in George H. Drury's *Guide to North American Steam Locomotives: History and Development of Steam Power since 1900* (Waukesha, Wis.: Kalmbach Publishing Co., 2000), pp. 124–129. For more detailed information, consult *Rock Island Steam Power,* by J. Wesley Krambeck, William D. Edson, and Jack W. Farrell (Potomac, Md.: Edson Publications, 2002), and *Rock Island Motive Power, 1933–1955,* by the late Lloyd E. Stagner (Boulder, Colo.: Pruett Publishing Co., 1980).

Stagner's "In 4-8-4s, If Not in Finance, Rock Island Excelled," *Trains* 40, no. 5 (March 1981), pp. 20–35, is a model study of a single-engine class.

Diesel Oddities

The final word on the Rock's diesel fleet is Louis A. Marre's *Rock Island Diesel Locomotives, 1930–1980* (Cincinnati, Ohio: Railfax, Inc. 1982). J. David Ingles' "Christine and the Mongeese," *Trains* 26, no. 2 (December 1965), pp. 28–39, brings order to the Rock's very untidy diesel roster.

Rebuilding the Rock

Willard V. Anderson's "Rebirth of a Railroad," *Trains* 8, no. 2 (December 1947), pp. 22–29, details almost mile by mile the renewal of Rock's aging infrastructure. Wallace W. Abbey's "Samson of the Cimarron," *Trains and Travel* 12, no. 8 (June 1952), pp. 48–49, recounts one of the major engineering achievements of that renewal.

5. The Road to Ride

The passenger-friendly Rock Island is documented train-by-train in Greg Stout's *Route of the Rockets: Rock Island in the Streamlined Era* (Hart, Mo.: White River Productions, 1997).

Trains magazine (briefly *Trains and Travel* from 1951 to 1953) is the best year-to-year source of information on the ups and downs of Rock's passenger and commuter business. "He Didn't Know It Couldn't Be Done," by Nancy Fords, *Trains and Travel,* 13, no. 4 (February 1953), pp. 18–21, tells of the road's drastic measures to control dining-car losses.

Early experiments with "restaurant cars" are recounted in Hayes, *Iron Road to Empire,* pp. 91–92. For contemporary accounts of the birth of the *Rocket* streamliner fleet, see "Rocket Trains Win Traffic," *Modern Railroads* 7, no. 10 (October 1952), pp. 53–58, and "The Spectacular 'Rockets,'" *Railway Age,* 133, no. 14 (October 6, 1952), pp. 111–115.

Arthur D. Dubin tells the sad story of the stillborn *Golden Rocket* in *Some Classic Trains* (Milwaukee: Kalmbach Publishing Co. 1964), pp. 213–221.

Commuterville

For a detailed overview of Rock Island and its commuters, see "A History of the Suburban Service of the Rock Island Railroad in the Chicago Area," by Robert E. Stewart Jr., *Bulletin 77* (July 1949) of the Railway and Locomotive Historical Society, pp. 34–66.

Though it doesn't deal with Rock Island specifically, Ann Durkin Keating's "Commuter Suburbs of the Railroad Age," chapter 5, *Chicagoland: City and Suburbs in the Railroad Age* (Chicago: University of Chicago Press, 2005), pp. 93–113, presents a useful background to the railroads' role in the movement to the suburbs; see also Hayes, *Iron Road to Empire,* pp. 91–92.

The Limon Do-Si-Do

The daily combination and recombination of the Rocky Mountain Rocket, witnessed many times by this author, is explained step-by-step in "Where the Rockets Wed," by Earl Cochran, *Trains and Travel* 13, no. 6 (April 1953), pp. 65–67.

6. The Road to Ruin

Many have analyzed Rock Island's fall from grace. Richard Saunders Jr.'s *Merging Lines: America's Railroads, 1900–1970* (DeKalb: Northern Illinois University Press, 2001), sets that fall in the context of the mad scramble for merger partners that escalated in the 1960s. "Stalemate in the West, 1963–1970," chapter 12, pp. 321–353, is particularly useful.

Rock Island's troubles and prospects from the Union Pacific's point of view are taken up in detail in Maury Klein's *Union Pacific: The Reconfiguration: America's Greatest Railroad from 1969 to the Present* (New York: Oxford University Press, 2011).

Trains magazine's month-to-month chronicle of the railroad's final years is informative, if painful, reading. John W. Ingram's "Notes on the Demise of the Chicago, Rock Island & Pacific," in the magazine's September 1980 issue (40, no. 11), provides a rueful postmortem by one of the men who tried to save the Rock.

Another man who fought to save the Rock is the subject of H. Roger Grant's excellent biography, *Visionary Railroader: Jervis Langdon Jr. and the Transportation Revolution* (Bloomington: Indiana University Press, 2008). In *Encyclopedia of North American Railroads,* David C. Lester profiles the equally visionary John W. Barriger III., pp. 167–169, and Downing Jenks, who began the Rock's search for a merger partner, pp. 566–567.

Epilogue: Pieces of the Rock

Richard J. Lane, the former Rock Island employee charged with the responsibility of disposing of the pieces of the Rock, recalls this melancholy task in "Liquidating the Rock," *Railroad History,* Bulletin 181 (Autumn 1999) of the Railway and Locomotive Historical Society, pp. 103–115. Maury Klein outlines Union Pacific's share of the leftovers in *Union Pacific: The Reconfiguration,* chapter 20, pp. 267–279.

Steve Glischinski takes up the story of the Iowa Interstate, pp. 75–87, and Rail America's Kyle Railroad, pp. 89–94, in *Regional Railroads of the Midwest* (St. Paul, Minn.: Voyageur Press/MBI Publishing Co. 2007). Jerome P. Lipka, president and CEO of Iowa Interstate, acknowledged that road's ties to the past in a phone conversation, May 24, 2012.

Most other "Regionals" now doing business on former Rock Island lines have their own websites, though names change and some operations that are here today may be gone tomorrow.

RESOURCES

The history and lore of Rock Island has been richly served by two excellent magazines, *Remember the Rock,* published since 2004 by Andover Junction Publications (http://www.andoverjunction.com), and Rock Island Technical Society's *Rocket.* The society (http://www.rits. org) also publishes the *Digest,* an irregular compendium of all things pertaining to Rock Island.

Sadly, the only general history of the road, William Edward Hayes' *Iron Road to Empire* (New York: Simmons-Boardman), was published in 1953, when Rock Island still had many useful miles to run. Richard Saunders Jr. tells much of what happened afterward in *Merging Lines: American Railroads, 1900–1970* (DeKalb: Northern Illinois University Press, 2001). Bill Fahrenwald's essay on Rock Island in the *Encyclopedia of North American Railroads* (Bloomington: Indiana University Press, 2007), edited by William D. Middleton, George M. Smerk, and Roberta L. Diehl, is a must-read, as is "Notes on the Demise of the Chicago, Rock Island & Pacific," by John W. Ingram, in the September 1980 issue of *Trains* (vol. 40, no. 11).

Useful geographic studies of the Rock's place in the scheme of things include *Iowa Railroads,* by Frank P. Donovan Jr. (Iowa City: University of Iowa Press, 2000); *Steel Trails of Hawkeyeland: Iowa's Railroad Experience,* by Don L. Hofsommer (Bloomington: Indiana University Press, 2005); *The Iron Horse and the Windy City: How Railroads Shaped Chicago,* by David M. Young (DeKalb: Northern Illinois University Press, 2003); *Chicagoland: City and Suburbs in the Railway Age,* by Ann Durkin Keating (Chicago: University of Chicago Press, 2005); *Railroads in Oklahoma,* edited by Donovan L. Hofsommer (Oklahoma City: Oklahoma Historical Society, 1977); *New Mexico's Railroads: An Historical Survey,* by David Myrick (Golden: Colorado Railroad Museum, 1970); "Rocketing to the Rockies," by Michael C. Doty and E. M. "Mel" McFarland, in *Colorado Rail Annual No. 17* (Golden: Colorado Railroad Museum, 1987); and *The Rock Island in Minnesota,* by John C. Luecke (St. Paul, Minn.: Grenadier Publications, 2011). For the Lone Star State, consult entries for "Chicago, Rock Island and Pacific Railroad," "Rock Island System," "Burlington-Rock Island Railroad," and "Chicago, Rock Island and Gulf Railway" in the *Handbook of Texas,* online at http://www.tshaonline.org/handbook/search/results/field.

Finally, for a sense of what it was like to work for Rock Island in its last days, read *Terminal Tales: Memories of a Chicago Div. Trainmaster,* by J. Pete Hedgpeth (Newton, Iowa: C.P.M., 2004).

INDEX

Italicized page numbers indicate illustrations or photos.

BOOKS IN THE RAILROADS PAST AND PRESENT SERIES:

Landmarks on the Iron Road: Two Centuries of North American Railroad Engineering by William D. Middleton

South Shore: The Last Interurban (revised second edition) by William D. Middleton

Katy Northwest: The Story of a Branch Line Railroad by Don L. Hofsommer

"Yet there isn't a train I wouldn't take": Railway Journeys by William D. Middleton by William D. Middleton

The Pennsylvania Railroad in Indiana by William J. Watt

In the Traces: Railroad Paintings of Ted Rose by Ted Rose

A Sampling of Penn Central: Southern Region on Display by Jerry Taylor

The Lake Shore Electric Railway Story by Herbert H. Harwood Jr. and Robert S. Korach

The Pennsylvania Railroad at Bay: William Riley McKeen and the Terre Haute & Indianapolis Railroad by Richard T. Wallis

The Bridge at Québec by William D. Middleton

History of the J. G. Brill Company by Debra Brill

Uncle Sam's Locomotives: The USRA and the Nation's Railroads by Eugene L. Huddleston

Metropolitan Railways: Rapid Transit in America by William D. Middleton

Perfecting the American Steam Locomotive by J. Parker Lamb

From Small Town to Downtown: A History of the Jewett Car Company, 1893–1919 by Lawrence A. Brough and James H. Graebner

Limiteds, Locals, and Expresses in Indiana, 1838-1971 by Craig Sanders

Steel Trails of Hawkeyeland: Iowa's Railroad Experience by Don L. Hofsommer

Amtrak in the Heartland by Craig Sanders

When the Steam Railroads Electrified (revised second edition) by William D. Middleton

The GrandLuxe Express: Traveling in High Style by Karl Zimmermann

Still Standing: A Century of Urban Train Station Design by Christopher Brown

The Indiana Rail Road Company: America's New Regional Railroad by Christopher Rund

Evolution of the American Diesel Locomotive by J. Parker Lamb

The Men Who Loved Trains: The Story of Men Who Battled Greed to Save an Ailing Industry by Rush Loving Jr.

The Train of Tomorrow by Ric Morgan

Built to Move Millions: Streetcar Building in Ohio by Craig R. Semsel

The CSX Clinchfield Route in the 21st Century by Jerry Taylor and Ray Poteat

The New York, Westchester & Boston Railway: J. P. Morgan's Magnificent Mistake by Herbert H. Harwood Jr.

Iron Rails in the Garden State: Tales of New Jersey Railroading by Anthony J. Bianculli

Visionary Railroader: Jervis Langdon Jr. and the Transportation Revolution by H. Roger Grant

The Duluth South Shore & Atlantic Railway: A History of the Lake Superior District's Pioneer Iron Ore Hauler by John Gaertner

Iowa's Railroads: An Album by H. Roger Grant and Don L. Hofsommer

Frank Julian Sprague: Electrical Inventor and Engineer by William D. Middleton and William D. Middleton III

Twilight of the Great Trains (expanded edition) by Fred W. Frailey

Little Trains to Faraway Places by Karl Zimmermann

Railroad Noir: The American West at the End of the Twentieth Century by Linda Grant Niemann

From Telegrapher to Titan: The Life of William C. Van Horne by Valerie Knowles

The Railroad That Never Was: Vanderbilt, Morgan, and the South Pennsylvania Railroad by Herbert H. Harwood Jr.

Boomer: Railroad Memoirs by Linda Grant Niemann

Indiana Railroad Lines by Graydon M. Meints

The Indiana Rail Road Company: America's New Regional Railroad (revised and expanded edition) by Christopher Rund, Fred W. Frailey, and Eric Powell

The CSX Clinchfield Route in the 21st Century (now in paperback) by Jerry Taylor and Ray Poteat

Wet Britches and Muddy Boots: A History of Travel in Victorian America by John H. White Jr.

Landmarks on the Iron Road: Two Centuries of North American Railroad Engineering (now in paperback) by William D. Middleton

On Railways Far Away by William D. Middleton

Railroads of Meridian by J. Parker Lamb, with contributions by David H. Bridges and David S. Price

Railroads and the American People by H. Roger Grant

The Electric Pullman: A History of the Niles Car and Manufacturing Company by Lawrence A. Brough

John Frank Stevens: Civil Engineer by Clifford Foust

Off the Main Line: A Photographic Odyssey by Don L. Hofsommer

A longtime observer of the Rock Island, both trackside and onboard, **Bill Marvel** has been a newspaper journalist and freelance writer for 49 years. His work has appeared in many publications, including *Smithsonian, Horizon, American Way, American Heritage Invention & Technology, D Magazine, 5280, Southwest Spirit,* and *TWA's Ambassador*. He is author (with R. V. Burgin) of *Islands of the Damned: A Marine at War in the Pacific,* a main selection of the History Book Club. He is currently working on a narrative history of the 1913–14 Colorado coal war.